*Your Fondest Annie*

## CLASSICS OF IRISH HISTORY
*General Editor:* Tom Garvin

Original publication dates of reprinted titles are given in brackets

P. S. O'Hegarty, *The Victory of Sinn Féin* (1924)
Walter McDonald, *Some Ethical Questions of Peace and War* (1919)
Joseph Johnston, *Civil War in Ulster* (1913)
James Mullin, *The Story of a Toiler's Life* (1921)
Robert Brennan, *Ireland Standing Firm* and *Eamon de Valera* (1958)
Mossie Harnett, *Victory and Woe:*
*The West Limerick Brigade in the War of Independence*
Padraig de Burca and John F. Boyle, *Free State or Republic?*
*Pen Pictures of the Historic Treaty Session of Dáil Éireann* (1922)
Arthur Clery, *The Idea of a Nation* (1907)
Standish James O'Grady, *To the Leaders of Our Working People*
Michael Davitt, *Jottings in Solitary*
Oliver MacDonagh, *Ireland: The Union and its Aftermath* (1977)
Thomas Fennell, *The Royal Irish Constabulary:*
*A History and Personal Memoir*
Arthur Griffith, *The Resurrection of Hungary* (1918)
William McComb, *The Repealer Repulsed* (1841)
George Moore, *Parnell and His Island* (1887)
Charlotte Elizabeth Tonna, *Irish Recollections*
(1841/47 as *Personal Recollections*)
Standish James O'Grady, *Sun and Wind*
John Sarsfield Casey, *The Galtee Boy: A Fenian Prison Narrative*
William and Mary Ann Hanbidge,
*Memories of West Wicklow: 1813–1939* (1939)
A. P. A. O'Gara, *The Green Republic* (1902)
William Cooke Taylor, *Reminiscences of Daniel O'Connell* (1847)
William Bruce and Henry Joy, *Belfast Politics* (1794)
Annie O'Donnell, *Your Fondest Annie*
John Mitchel, *The Last Conquest of Ireland (Perhaps)* (1858/9)
Joseph Keating, *My Struggle for Life* (1916)
Harold Begbie, *The Lady Next Door* (1912) (*forthcoming*)

# *Your Fondest Annie*

Letters from Annie O'Donnell to James P. Phelan
1901–1904

ANNIE O'DONNELL

*edited by Maureen Murphy*

UNIVERSITY COLLEGE DUBLIN PRESS
Preas Choláiste Ollscoile Bhaile Átha Cliath

This edition first published by
University College Dublin Press 2005

© Francis Phelan 2005
Introduction and notes © Maureen Murphy 2005

ISBN 1-904558-37-2
ISSN 1393-6883

University College Dublin Press
Newman House, 86 St Stephen's Green
Dublin 2, Ireland
*www.ucdpress.ie*

Cataloguing in Publication data
available from the British Library

Typeset in Ireland in Ehrhardt by
Elaine Shiels, Bantry, Co. Cork
Text design by Lyn Davies,
Frome, Somerset, England
Printed in England on acid-free paper
by Antony Rowe Ltd

# CONTENTS

*Note on the Text*

The text of the letters has been typeset from Annie O'Donnell's previously unpublished letters which were kept in the Phelan family. The text has been as little altered as possible, with only very minor modifications made to spelling and punctuation. Round brackets where used are those of Annie O'Donnell; square brackets indicate the editor's additions or corrections. Annie occasionally crossed through a word which has been reproduced in the printed letters.

# INTRODUCTION

*Maureen Murphy*

In October 1898, eighteen-year-old Annie O'Donnell left her home in the townland of Lippa, near Spiddal, County Galway to go to America. She and the other 15,175 Irish women who left that year were a phenomenon in European migration; they outnumbered their 9,952 male emigrant counterparts by twenty per cent (60.39 per cent to 39.60 per cent).[1] Like most of her contemporaries, Annie went into domestic service. While Annie's work life may have been a happier one than that of other household servants, her experiences of separation, adaptation and acculturation were similar to many of her contemporaries. Their full story has yet to be told.

Pioneering studies of Irish women's emigration like Hasia Diner's *Erin's Daughters in America: Irish Immigrant Women in the Nineteenth Century* (1983) and Janet Nolan's *Ourselves Alone: Women's Emigration from Ireland 1885–1920* (1989) provide statistical and anecdotal information about domestic servants. Faye E. Dudden's *Serving Women: Household Service in Nineteenth-Century America* (1983) includes the experience of Irish women in her analysis of domestic service, and Mona Hearn's *Below Stairs: Domestic Service Remembered in Dublin and Beyond, 1880–1922* (1993) examines the lives of Irish domestics who stayed in Ireland when Annie and her contemporaries emigrated. Annie's letters represent a unique contribution to this literature because they provide a sustained three-year narrative of her life as a children's nurse in Pittsburgh at the turn of the twentieth century.

Annie O'Donnell was born on 7 or 8 May 1880 in the townland of Lippa near Spiddal, a small village twelve miles west of Galway City.[2] The years 1879–80 brought another, less well-known, famine to Galway and to Connemara's precarious economy.[3] In 1881, Lippa's 388 acres supported a dozen houses and a population of 84 persons. Annie was the second youngest child, the fifth daughter, of Patrick O'Donnell and Margaret Concannon.[4] She was baptised in St Enda's Church on 10 May by Rev. William Wilson who was to die later in a local typhoid epidemic; Annie's sponsors appear to have been an aunt and uncle: Ellen Concannon and Martin O'Donnell.

The 1884 Spiddal parish census lists the O'Donnell children before emigration scattered the family: Bridget (19), Pat (16), Mary (13), Kate (no age given), Honor (8), Margaret (6) Anne (3) and John (1½). (Since Annie would have been five, not three, in 1884, the children's ages may reflect reported rather than actual dates.) Bridget emigrated in 1888; Mary followed two years later.

Did Bridget follow her neighbour Patrick Lydon to Pittsburgh? Had he joined the flood of immigrant labourers from Connemara who emigrated to Pittsburgh to work in the city's coal mines, steel mills and glass factories?[5]

In language that reminds the reader of lines from the traditional emigration song 'Thousands are Sailing' and Liam O'Flaherty's short story 'Going into Exile', Annie's letter of 5 May 1902 speaks of the aching sadness of children leaving home:

> I believe my youngest brother will soon come here too. He is only a young lad about 18. Then the old homestead will be rid of us all excepting my oldest brother. Is it not too bad to see such a sad scene? As soon as a boy or girl gets big enough to help the house, he is forced to

leave perhaps never again to see those dear ones and would give anything in after years for one hour of that innocent happy fun known only
in their dear old homes. (p. 65)[6]

Lippa and Spiddal, part of the region known as Cois Fharraige, the
foot of the sea, the Irish-speaking district west of Galway city, was
an area of high emigration driven by local poverty. Maud Wynne
spent childhood summers at Spiddal House, the demesne of her
father Michael Morris, Lord Killanin, the Catholic Unionist MP
for Galway who served later as Chief Justice of Ireland from 1887 to
1889. In her memoir, Wynne described the region's fragile economy
in the early decades of the twentieth century:

> The potatoes rotten and the turf not saved were two dreaded possibil-
> ities too close to our childhood. There, between the Atlantic Ocean on
> one side and an interminable bog on the other, lay a narrow strip of
> possible cultivation, at its widest it was never more than one mile and a
> half, and on that strip, amidst the rocks and heather, lived a most
> prolific population. It was one of the most congested districts in Ireland.
> There were in truth only some sacks of potatoes and dried turf between
> the people and starvation, for the turf was sold in Galway to buy meal
> and other necessaries of life.[7]

John Millington Synge observed Spiddal's poverty in 1905
when he walked through the congested districts with the painter
Jack B. Yeats. He wrote 'that it is part of the misfortune of Ireland
that nearly all the characteristics which give colour and attractive-
ness to Irish life are bound up with a social condition that is near
to penury'.[8] Stephen Gwynn, Nationalist MP for Galway City
(1906–18), reflected on the bleak coastal landscape: a grey sky, black
curraghs close to the shingle beach in *A Holiday in Connemara*
(1909) concluding that it was American remittances that provided
the rent for the local landlords.[9]

While there was a narrow margin between economic want and sufficiency, Annie looked back on her childhood spent along Galway Bay with unwavering nostalgia for 'the many happy days I spent by its waters in dear old Galway, and for one such day would now give almost anything' (p. 39). Years later, in his short story 'Lonely House Now', Annie's son Frank Phelan recalled his conversation with his mother when she visited him in Washington before his ordination to the priesthood.

> If you ever go to Galway – I'm sure you will – ask to be shown 'The Silver Strand'. It is all changed now, but there when I was a girl it was my favorite place. It was all lonely, and I went down to it at night. The sand made it shine, and the sparkle of the periwinkles in the brine. There was a song we children sang – and we danced to it. And she told me of it: how the girls would sing a verse about things of long gone by, how they were there for a while but are gone – how nothing is left. It was in Irish, and she showed me there in the corner of the restaurant how the girls pirouetted.
>
> I only remember parts of it, but I remember those clearly, for she repeated the Irish for it, and each refrain ended with the rending cry, 'O Lord, let something remain!' It is the way I remember her, singing that: 'O Lord, let something remain'.[10]

Annie's early education was at the local National School in Spiddal. She later told her daughters how her sister Honor carried her over the streams. It is likely Domhnall Ó Duibhne (Daniel Deeney) was the national schoolteacher in the boys' school in Annie's time. He published *Peasant Lore from Gaelic Ireland* in 1900, a collection of folklore from the Spiddal area and from Donegal.[11] While most schoolteachers in Irish-speaking areas focused on preparing their pupils for emigration, Ó Duibhne would have encouraged all of the local school children to cherish their Irish language and oral tradition.

Unlike most Connemara girls, Annie was educated beyond National School standard. Her parents had special plans for their youngest daughter. They sent Annie at the age of sixteen to the teacher-training programme offered by the Presentation convent school in Galway.[12] When Annie arrived to enrol on 17 August 1896, the tall, dark-haired twelve-year-old portress who opened the convent door was Nora Barnacle, the woman who would run off with James Joyce to Europe eight years later.[13] Annie no doubt might have noticed the cast in Nora's left eye and her firm, straight mouth. That chance encounter had its own reverberations decades later when Annie's son Frank taught courses in James Joyce's fiction to a generation of students at Notre Dame University and at Stonehill College.

An old school roll book in the Presentation Convent archives records that Annie left the Presentations on 16 April 1898. During her almost two years at the Presentation Sisters' school (17 August 1896–16 April 1898), Annie studied reading, writing, arithmetic, spelling, grammar, geography, needlework and drawing (for which additional fees were charged). She did not take classes in cooking, laundry or music (vocal or instrumental). The Galway Presentation Sisters utilised the monitorial system in their teacher-training programme.

> The monitorial system was a mode of teaching in which older pupils were responsible for supervising and teaching younger ones. The mutual system, as the method was also styled, was in use for some years before it gained widespread acceptance in the classroom. Lack of money coupled with acute shortage of experienced teachers were the principal factors responsible for the spread of the system.[14]

Annie did not board with the Presentation Sisters; she was a day-girl who probably stayed with the Concannons, her mother's family, who lived in Léana Riabhach, the townland just west of Annie's beloved Silver Strand. Léana Riabhach was within walking distance of the Presentation Sisters' School in Rahoon.

A native Irish speaker who had completed training as a monitor in a school that supported the teaching of Irish, Annie applied optimistically for the position of schoolmistress on Inishmore; however, according to family tradition, the parish priest favoured a niece of his own.[15] There is probably more than family loyalty here. Father Murtagh Faragher, who managed the three islands' ten schools, was high-handed even for the autocratic standards of the day. His long-standing feud with the Oatquarter Boys' School (Inishmore) schoolmaster David O'Callaghan is the subject of Liam O'Flaherty's novel *Skerrett*. (In the novel when Skerrett, the schoolmaster, and his wife arrive on Nara [Aran], Kate Skerrett thanks Father Moclair for Skerrett's appointment saying, 'We'd have to go to America . . . only for you giving us this school.')[16]

On the other hand, Annie's lack of musical training would have been a liability as national schoolteachers were expected to teach their pupils the music for church liturgies and processions and to train the choir.[17] With little hope of finding a teaching job in Ireland, Annie decided to join her older sisters Bridget and Mary in Pittsburgh.

There is no record of Annie's departure. Did she have an American wake and the kind of leave-taking from her family and neighbours that her younger Spiddal neighbour Máirtín Ó Cadhain describes in 'The Year 1912', his emigration story of a Connemara girl told with tenderness from the point of view of the mother mute with the anguish of loss?[18] What did Annie pack in her trunk? Did her mother Margaret O'Donnell have forebodings about the hardships ahead of Annie? Did she accept the loss of a third daughter to America with a resigned, 'God is good'?

Data from the records of 1,488 women who left Queenstown earlier, in April 1898, indicate that 30 per cent of those emigrants travelled with siblings, relatives and neighbours. Of the cohort, 12.5 per cent were identified as Non-Immigrant Aliens, Irish women who had worked in America, visited home and were returning to the United States. Records of places of origin and destinations suggest that the returners often acted as escorts for the emigrating siblings, relatives and friends. It is possible that Annie might have travelled with Kittie Hentey, aged 26, the only other Queenstown passenger from Galway who was 'returning home' to her sister Mrs Fahy in Philadelphia. Like the 37.93 per cent of the April 1898 cohort, Annie was going to sisters in America.[19]

What we do know is that Annie left Queenstown on 28 October 1898 aboard the Hamburg-American steamer *Adria* (1896) bound for Philadephia. Phelan family tradition describes the *Adria* as an old tramp steamer. In fact, it was just two years old; however, compared with other liners on the North American run like the White Star's *Cymric* (1898), it was undersized and overcrowded. The 5,458-ton *Adria* was 399.3 ft long, had one funnel, two masts and travelled at 13 knots while the 13,096 ton *Cymric* was 585 ft, had one funnel, four masts and a speed of 14.5 knots. Despite the difference in size, the steerage accommodations were remarkably similar: 1,100 on the *Adria* and 1,160 on the *Cymric*. (The *Cymric* carried 258 first-class passengers to the *Adria's* twenty.)[20]

On the tender going out to the ship, Annie addressed Jim Phelan, a 22-year-old farmer from Kildrinagh, near Urlingford, County Kilkenny who had run away from home during Sunday mass to join his uncle Joseph Brennan, a tilesetter in Indianapolis.[21] Annie and Jim were part of a circle of other young people travelling in the group, 24 Irish passengers who boarded at Queenstown. In the course of their fortnight's journey, Annie and Jim became friends.

Annie mentions two other Jims from their group in her letters to Jim Phelan: 'Galway Jim' and 'Mayo Jim'. 'Galway Jim' Butler was a 20-year-old mechanic from Tuam en route to his brother Thomas in Philadephia. 'Mayo Jim' Murray (aged 22), a labourer, travelled with his widowed mother Sarah (aged 50); both were illiterate. 'Mayo Jim' had brothers and a sister in Pittsburgh.[22]

Annie later recalled her seasickness and frightening moments in the stormy North Atlantic crossing, but she mainly spoke of the fun that included a Halloween celebration which lacked apples for bobbing, but no doubt featured singing, dancing and traditional divination games (p. 46). When they arrived in Philadelphia on 10 November, Annie O'Donnell and Jim Phelan's names were listed consecutively on the *Adria*'s manifest.

Annie indicated that she was going to her sister Bridget and that she had $10. Jim may have intended to go first to New York because the name of the city had been crossed out and Pa. written over it. There was also the notation 'bound to cousins'; however, Annie and Jim travelled together with the Murrays by train from Philadelphia to Pittsburgh. Annie delighted Mrs Murray by talking with her in Irish. Later she wished she had paid more attention to her (p. 55). When they parted at Union Station, Pittsburgh, Jim Phelan scribbled the address of Annie's sister Bridget on a timetable – P. Lydon, rear of 1225 Liberty Street.[23]

At the station, Annie and her sisters failed to recognise each other. In some ways, it augured a more serious lack of connection. When Annie later described her first months in the city to Jim, she recalled bitterly the lonely and discouraging weeks and the feeling that she was not welcomed by her sisters.[24] Bridget left Ireland when Annie was eight; Mary followed Bridget when Annie was ten. By 1898, Bridget and Mary had married railway labourers Patrick Lydon and Patrick Keady and were struggling to raise their own young families in tenements across from Union Station. The sisters may have felt that Annie would be an additional responsibility and drain on their already strained resources (pp. 44, 83).

Annie's reception taught her that life was duty and that she could survive in America only by becoming independent and by being reserved in her manner (p. 37). Her experience may have deepened her natural melancholy, and her letters reveal a tendency to expect the worst or to feel that life was meant to disappoint her.[25] She also shared the fatalism of Irish countrywomen who believed that they must accept what heaven sent.[26]

By contrast, Jim was optimistic and cheerful; Annie called him 'the life of the *Adria*' (p. 46). In her letter of 17 July 1903, Annie enclosed a poem about another sunny Jim by Edwin L. Sabin called 'Trouble-Proof' that she clipped from *Lippencott's*. It begins:

> Never rains where Jim is –
> People kickin' whinin'
> He goes round insistin'
> 'Sun is almost shinin!'(p. 106)

Even the environment was depressing to Annie, for nothing could have been further from the Galway sea and sky Annie left than Pittsburgh in 1898. While Pittsburgh was the world centre for iron and steel production, by 1900 industrialisation brought soot and dirt. The hills around the city had been levelled in order to mine the soft coal that gave Pittsburgh the name Annie called it, 'Smoky City'. She also suffered from the heat in the summer which further increased the soot and grit. Later, when Annie became accustomed to smoke and grime, she worried that Jim might not like the city; she urged him to think instead of the work opportunities that Pittsburgh offered (p. 104). It was an attitude Annie would have heard expressed in the Mellon household.

With her good education, Annie herself found employment almost immediately taking care of Colonel James and Rebecca

Schoonmaker's children in Vollenhouse, their home at 4940 Ellsworth Avenue in Pittsburgh's suburban Shadyside neighbourhood.[27] This was Annie's introduction to Pittsburgh's industrial elite and to the world of the city's art collectors who decorated their Victorian mansions with the work of continental artists like Georges-Jean-Marie (1854–1906) whose *Steering Lesson* was loaned by Colonel Schoonmaker to the Carnegie Library Club Exhibition of 1895.[28]

According to her children, Annie had worked for the Schoonmakers for seven months until the summer of 1899 when the Colonel died and Mrs Schoonmaker decided to return to her own people in the South (p. 37). In fact Colonel Schoonmaker lived till 1927. Perhaps the Schoonmaker children outgrew their children's nurse, and Mrs Schoonmaker tried to find a new position for Annie. (According to the 1910 census, James Jr was twelve and Gretchen was four in 1899.) She recommended Annie to her Shadyside neighbour Mrs W. L. Mellon who was looking for a children's nurse.[29] Though her mother was Irish, Mrs Mellon was hesitant about hiring an Irish girl, but, according to Annie's daughter Eulalia, Mrs Schoonmaker was said to have advised her, 'Don't make any decisions till you hear this girl. She speaks the King's English.'

Annie obviously made a good impression on young Mrs Mellon, because she moved around the corner from Vollenhouse in the late summer or fall of 1899 to join the staff in the broad, stone, three-storey house at 4616 Bayard Street near the corner of North Craig Street (p. 30). She was 19. A devout Catholic who believed that God's hand was in all things, Annie considered it providential that she became a 'Mellon girl'.

> I think I was a fortunate girl the day I got into this family, for it is one of the best houses in the City. They are kind and will never let a small thing done for them go unrewarded, so it is a pleasure to work for them. (p. 68)

Later that year, she again counted being with the Mellons a blessing, 'Heaven sent me to that big stone house' (p. 83).

Her employer William Larimer Mellon (1869–1949) was the son of James Ross Mellon and Rachel Larimer Mellon; Andrew Mellon was his uncle. W. L. would make his own fortune when he founded, with other Pittsburgh businessmen, the Gulf Oil Corporation in January 1907. Scottish-born Mary 'May' Taylor Mellon (1872–1942) emigrated to the Unites States in 1894. She married W. L. Mellon in 1896.

Annie was engaged as one of two children's maids for Matthew (b. 1897) and Rachel (b. 1899).[30] A third child Margaret was born in 1901, and a second son, William L. (Larry), arrived in 1910. By then Annie had left the family. The household staff was a large one. The 1900 census lists four servants: a nurse Ellen Comphreys (29), and three maids: Rose Wiener (27), Mary O'Neill (45) and Annie O'Donnell (20).[31] Mrs Walters, the housekeeper, is not listed in the report nor is the cook. The Mellons also employed two coachmen. Annie's favourite companion was Ellen Comphreys, an English Catholic of Irish parents. Almost ten years older than Annie, Ellen became her closest friend, confidante and perhaps her surrogate mother.[32]

When the Mellon children outgrew their nurses, Ellen went to New York to look after two little girls the same age as Annie's older girls. In her later years, Ellen returned to Pittsburgh and was as solicitous as ever about Annie. A frequent visitor to the Phelan household, Annie's son Frank describes Ellen as a short, stout, elegantly dressed woman. Old-fashioned in her ways, she was nonetheless someone who 'knew who she was'.[33]

Annie not only felt herself fortunate in her friendship with Ellen, but her letters are also full of her gratitude for Mrs Mellon's many kindnesses to her and to the other girls. May Mellon made sure her staff had the best medical care (p. 63); she fixed up the

porch for a summer dining room and place to socialise on hot
summer evenings (p. 67); she gave them compensatory time off and
pay when they had extra duties such as Annie and Ellen's travels with
the children (pp. 62, 72, 79); she arranged treats like theatre outings
for her girls (pp. 50, 87); she brought them little presents from her
travels (p. 79), and she gave thoughtful gifts at holidays (p. 90).

A religious woman who preferred the doings of the Shadyside
Presbyterian Church to the social life of her wealthy Mellon in-
laws, her son Larry, who became a medical missionary in Haiti,
called his mother 'the great spiritual force in my life'.[34] Mrs Mellon
saw to it that the Mellon girls went to mass not only on Sundays
but on First Fridays, a popular Catholic devotion to the Sacred
Heart that promised the grace of final repentance to those who
receive communion on nine consecutive first Fridays. Like their
New England counterparts, the Presbyterian Mellons, particularly
the older generations, may have held anti-Catholic views, but this
did not deter them from hiring Irish Catholic women to look after
their children.

Like other Victorian homes in Shadyside, the Mellon children's
nursery was on the second floor. Annie and Ellen did not have rooms
on the top floor like the rest of the maids; they lived with the children. At night, while the children slept, the room was their own and
they sat by the fire sewing, talking and drinking cups of tea.[35]

Since the Mellons had a large household staff, Annie's duties
were centred on the children. When they were in Pittsburgh, she
rose early with the children, washed and dressed them, buttoned
their boots, brushed and combed their hair, organised breakfast for
Matthew and Rachel, fed baby Margaret and then walked Matthew
back and forth to school. (She doesn't name the school, but it was
likely the neighbourhood Shady Side Academy at Ellsworth and
Morewood, across from the Schoonmaker's home or the Alinda
School at the corner of Fifth Avenue and Craig Street.)[36]

Annie and Ellen played with the little girls or took them for walks during the morning. They probably did not cook the children's meals but they supervised lunch and supper in the nursery. After lunch there were naps for the little girls while Annie walked back to Matthew's school. When they returned, Annie and Ellen took the children out to play in Schenley Park. There was supper in the nursery followed by baths, time with the Mellons, stories and bed. If Mrs Mellon were not in to say goodnight, Annie and Ellen would have said their evening prayers with them. Their work continued after they tucked the children in bed. While they probably did not have to do most of the children's laundry, they were responsible for their clothes. They mended tears and darned socks, and they made their own uniforms from the material supplied by May Mellon: white for the morning, black for the afternoon (p. 68). They sometimes had free time in the evenings to join the other help for a meal or some recreation. Their routine varied on weekend when Annie and Ellen took Matthew and Rachel to children's parties or special outings.

On Sundays, Annie and Ellen went to mass while the Mellons went to the Shadyside Presbyterian Church. They dressed the children in the best clothes for Sunday dinner when the Mellon grandparents and other relatives joined the family. Annie and Ellen often had Sunday afternoons free, and Annie sometimes visited her sisters. Her streetcar ride from Bayard Street to Libery Street was to travel from the space and comfort of Shadyside to the smoky inner city. From time to time Annie spoke of her concern about her tenure in the Mellon household. She knew, of course, that she would be replaced when the children outgrew their need for a nurse. While the Mellons had high standards for their staff, it was a happy household for the children. Matthew Mellon described his father as a man 'with a knack for fathering' his 'chickabiddies'. They grew up in luxury, but they were not spoilt. Matthew Mellon later recalled:

No escape was possible. We were locked in closets and spanked with hairbrushes when we offended the code; yet, we knew intuitively that our parents loved us and were doing it all for our good, which reminds me of an old hymn we sang down at the Presbyterian Church: Trust and obey; there's no other way.[37]

By Annie's accounts, it was a high-spirited household both above and below the stairs. Annie and the girls were given to practical jokes and a lot of good-natured teasing, and it appears that the Mellons too enjoyed the fun.[38]

Unlike the rest of the household staff, Annie and Ellen travelled with the Mellons. They summered in Spring Lake, a Victorian seaside resort on the New Jersey shore, and at Rachelwood, J. R. Mellon's baronial compound at Mt Florence near Ligonier in the Allegheny Mountains. Annie learned to ride a bicycle in Spring Lake, and she described the dances, hayrides and parties they enjoyed in the mountains in 1901 (p. 42). They spent winters in Florida aboard W. L. Mellon's large, paddle-wheel houseboat, the first of a series of increasingly luxurious yachts, all called *Vagabondia*, and at the Hotel Royal Palm in Miami. Because she travelled with the family, and lived in closer proximity than the housemaids, Annie identified closely with the Mellons whom she called 'our family' and 'our folks'.

It was on their summer holiday to Spring Lake in 1901, when Annie was 21, that Annie's sister Bridget forwarded a letter from Jim Phelan that reached her on 2 August (p. 35). It was the first Annie had heard from him since they had parted in Pittsburgh's Union Station three years earlier. He had become a streetcar man in Indianapolis, where he lived at 1719 N. Senate Avenue with his aunt and uncle the Joseph Brennans and with his sister Helena (Lena) whom Jim convinced to join them in 1899 (p. 36). Her letter to Jim, postmarked 6 August 1901, was the first of 70 letters that she wrote to him.

Was Annie being coy when she confessed she wasn't sure whether she remembered what Jim looked like, and begged him, as she had begged her parents, to send a photograph?[39] Photographs were part of the immigrant's ritual. As the mother in O'Cadhain's story 'The Year 1912' bids good-bye to her daughter, she says 'for the life of her, not to forget to have her picture taken beyond and send it home'.[40] And yet, as Eilís Dillon wrote in *The Bitter Glass*, the photographs were small compensation for their loss:

> It was dim comfort indeed to receive after a while unnatural photographs of strange young people with alien faces, dressed in peculiar American clothes. Fathers and brothers set to work to make large fretwork frames for, so that they could take their place on the mantelshelf and gradually fade into ghosts from the heat and the acid turf dust continually drifting over them.[41]

Annie treasured the images of her family and of Jim, and her enthusiasm for photographs did not escape Mrs Mellon's notice. She gave Annie the gift of a camera in 1902, and Annie became a keen photographer (pp. 60, 62, 79). Before his ill-fated marriage to Nora McMullen in 1900, W. L.'s uncle Andrew W. Mellon frequently visited the household to see the children during their evening play sessions with their parents.[42] A Phelan family story describes Annie asking A. W. Mellon in an informal moment during one of his visits whether she should invest some of her savings in Kodak. 'Keep your money, Annie', he cautioned, 'It's only a toy'.[43]

Jim's letter renewed their friendship, and their friendship deepened into a romance. Unusual among the Irish in America who generally met and 'walked out' at county or parish functions or through family and friends, Annie and Jim's was a courtship by correspondence. She signed her sixth letter with love, and the next letter finished with xxx. After his visit in the fall of 1902, the xxx line went right down the side of the page. Their letters reveal the hopes and plans of two young immigrants in their twenties at the turn of the century. They also reflect the emotional ups and downs of a young woman who lived from letter to letter. She enlisted other voices to talk to Jim about their future: Ellen's sympathetic encouragement; the other girls' teasing references to Jim; the children's curiosity about Jim's identity.

Annie's letters give some sense of the time constraints domestic help experienced even in a household as considerate and well staffed as the Mellon's. Annie usually wrote to Jim late at night when the children were settled in bed and after her other chores like mending and making her uniforms were finished. She never complained about her workday; however, as her friendship developed with Jim, she began to fret about how hard it was to make her own plans. When she visited New York with Mrs Mellon in December 1901, she was eager to meet Jim's cousins, but she didn't have time off.[44] When Jim's Uncle Joseph Brennan came to Pittsburgh on business and his daughter Pollie visited, Annie's letters were full of concern that she get the time off to meet and to entertain them (pp. 122–3). As she said in her letter of 5 November 1901, 'When I can not see *you*, the very least I may do is to see someone belonging to you.'

Annie was heartbroken when she was sent from Pittsburgh to New York with the children during the 1902 epidemic of measles and scarlet fever in Pittsburgh, a time that coincided with Jim's first visit to the city (p. 69). After she returned from the Mellons' summer visits to Spring Lake and Mt Florence, she had a week's vacation and Jim came to Pittsburgh from 28 September to 5 October.

Jim met the Mellon girls who 'never ceased talking about you, Jim' (p. 83). While Annie had promised Jim that he wouldn't have to push a baby carriage while he visited her (p. 81), they took the Mellon children on an outing to the Highland Park Zoo (p. 91). They visited the Lydons and the Keadys, probably on Sunday after mass at Shadyside's Sacred Heart Church. Jim rode the Pittsburgh streetcars. One day they travelled out to Westinghouse Avenue in East Pittsburgh perhaps to visit friends (p. 85). Mainly they talked and got to know each other again. The visit was a success. By the spring of 1903, he talked of coming to Pittsburgh to stay.

Some of Annie's 1902 letters spoke of her plan to become a nurse, but she abandoned the idea and chose to stay on with the Mellons until she left to marry Jim (pp. 54, 74). As her feelings for Jim deepened, her ambition shifted from her own future to his. While she always included the disclaimer, 'I leave it to you to decide. You know best', Annie persuaded Jim to move to Pittsburgh. She sent him news clippings about streetcar work in Pittsburgh including one entitled 'Streetcar Men get $30,000 Award for Careful Work' (6 Jan. 1903) (pp. 66, 92). Since Jim was an experienced Indianapolis streetcar man and W. L. Mellon's business interests included Pittsburgh's streetcars, Annie may have believed that she could have put a word in to help Jim get work.[45]

Jim also considered joining the fire department, and Annie encouraged him saying that she thought of him when she passed the local firehouse walking Matthew to school.[46] While she did not approve of the idea, Annie was so eager to see Jim succeed that she supported his brief career as a saloonkeeper. (Jim's children found a receipt for a barrel of whiskey among his papers, but he told his children that he didn't like what drink did to workingmen.)

Like most Irish servant girls, Annie sent money home. In 1903, she also supported the building campaign for the new church in Spiddal. Father Marcus Conroy, the parish priest, had gone house to house to get the addresses of family members in America who could contribute to the cost of the some £5,000 to build a new parish church – Cill Éinne (St Enda's). The Hiberno-Romanesque revival church was designed by William A. Scott who was described as the architect of the Celtic Renaissance.

Father Conroy's circular letter of 18 February 1903 appealed to Annie and other former parishioners in America. His mentioning countrywomen before countrymen may have been a subtle acknowledgment that it was the Irish women in America who had the reputation for giving generously to their churches.

> Unable to complete so great an undertaking by the slender resources of their poverty, the priest and people of Spiddal confidently appeal to the religious spirit of their countrywomen and countrymen at home and abroad to enable them to accomplish this great work for God.[47]

There may be a mythic element to claim that Irish servant girls built St Patrick's Cathedral in New York, but Annie's significant gift to the building fund was real. She forwarded $45.00 to Father Conroy; the amount represented five per cent of some $1,000 raised in America. Annie made her own donation; she collected money from the Mellon staff, and she enlisted Jim's help in soliciting funds in Indianapolis (p. 102).

The St Enda project renewed a link with home, so it is not surprising that Annie's letters to Jim describing her fundraising efforts often spoke, at the same time, of her yearning to go home again for a visit (p. 104). The passenger records of young women who worked in America, visited home and returned as 'non-immigrating aliens' suggest that four years was the usual time for that trip home.[48] For Annie, 1903, her fifth year in America, seemed to be the time she felt the urge to return most keenly.

Annie was further unsettled by Jim's moves between Indianapolis, Pittsburgh and Philadelphia during the winter of 1903–4. She was delighted when Jim sent her a ring for Christmas (p. 119). Annie did not mention what Jim said in his Christmas letter, so it is not clear whether he proposed to her; however, she took his intention seriously, but she was conflicted enough about leaving the household not to show the ring to Mrs Mellon. Her 1904 New Year's Day letter says that Mrs Mellon saw her ring for the first time that day, admired it but hoped that Annie would not marry immediately.

The year 1903 had been one of change for the Mellons. In August 1902, W. L. Mellon went to Beaumont, Texas, to take over the enterprise that would become Gulf Oil.[49] That success prompted Mellon to build his palatial Ben Elm, his 45-room mansion at the corner of Forbes Street and Darlington Road in the Squirrel Hill section of the city. While they were impressed with Ben Elm, Annie and Ellen were sad to leave their cosy nursery quarters on Bayard Street (p. 103). By then Annie was thinking about her own future with Jim. Like many Irish servant girls, Annie felt the pull of loyalty between that future and the children whom she regarded as very much her own.

Annie stayed on with the Mellons through the spring of 1904. She was part of the winter tour to Florida and returned with the Mellons to Pittsburgh towards the end of April. She wrote to Jim from the Hotel Royal Palm in Miami on 1 April describing their travel plans. While she tried to remain hopeful about her future, Annie's old pessimism returned during those months. She had pangs of loneliness about leaving the Mellon children; she worried about giving up her good job, and she was unsure about what her life would be with Jim.

Then, there is a gap in the letters until 7 June. Anticipating that Jim would come to Pittsburgh or that she would join him in Indianapolis, Annie left the Mellons. When Jim left the city abruptly for a couple of weeks, she panicked, sending telegrams and special delivery letters to Indianapolis. Her last letters are dated, but she gives no return address. The envelopes' postmarks from the East Liberty Station suggest that Annie was living in the area or at least visiting it regularly to check with Bridget to see if she had a letter from Jim. Ironically, the last address she gave Jim was the same one that she had written on the train schedule when they said good-bye in 1898 (p. 153).

Jim returned permanently to Pittsburgh and was living five houses from Perrysville Avenue on Charles Street in Allegheny which was a city until 1907 when it was absorbed into Pittsburgh. When they married in 1904 in the Church of the Epiphany, Ellen Comphreys was Annie's witness.[50] Annie and Jim spent their married life in the same northside part of the city. According to the census, by April 1910 the Phelans were settled on Dunlap Street off Perrysville Avenue. They lived first in a clapboard house at 427 Dunlap Street; in the late 1930s they moved up the hill to the two-storey brick house they built at 431. Jim did become the streetcar man that Annie planned. Her daughter Eileen said that Annie got him the job.

In the opening line of his story, 'The Breaking of the String', Jim's son Frank describes him as 'a streetcar man who wrote poetry between runs while he was waiting at the Keating barn on the north side of Pittsburgh'.[51] Jim never learned to drive a car, but he adapted to the change from horse-drawn streetcars to two generations of Pittsburgh's electric streetcars. Apart from a trolley strike in 1919, streetcar work was steady even during the Depression when Fr James Cox, Pastor of St Patrick's, led an army of Pittsburgh's unemployed to Washington in 1932.[52] Jim even had some extra money to invest. Like many Irish in America, he opted for property, four small lots and two double houses in the city's East End that he rented.

Irish women generally did not work after they married. In *Erin's Daughters in America*, Hasia R. Diner describes marriage as the end of an Irish-American woman's full-time work experience.

Upon marrying an Irish woman ended her life as a worker, as an earner of income. Although married Irish women worked for wage under

James P. Phelan in Pittsburgh, *c.*1930s

situations of duress – when their husbands were incapacitated or when they deserted – Irish wives generally had the lowest rate of employment.[53]

Some Irish domestic servants worked part-time or occasionally for their families. Annie did not stay in touch with the Mellons. A proud woman, her children said she didn't want Mrs Mellon to think she was looking for a handout, but one day in the 1930s a large parcel full of serving pieces – silver soup tureens and ladles – arrived from Ben Elm. A more lasting Mellon legacy was Annie's sensibility. There were standards in the Phelan household. If someone put a milk bottle on the table, Annie said, 'Take that bottle off the table. This isn't Mulligan's Flats'.[54]

While Irish immigrant women generally married less and later than other Americans, their birth rate was high. Annie, who had married young (24), had eight children, six of whom she and Jim raised to maturity: James (1905–10), John (1908–82), Mary Gertrude (1910–12), Kathleen (1912–2003), Eileen (1915–), Patricia (1918–2004), Eulalia (1921–) and Francis (1925–).

While Annie had a family of her own, she yearned to see her parents. She did go home again. When her eldest child James died at the age of five in 1910, Annie was heartbroken. Jim suggested she make that longed-for trip home with her children John and Mary Gertrude who was named after Sister Mary Gertrude Dooley, Annie's favourite nun at the Presentation Convent.[54] They sailed aboard the *Celtic* in June 1911.

The census taken earlier in the spring lists Patrick O'Donnell (84) as the head of household. Annie's mother was 71. Her brother Patrick (52) had been married four years to his wife Mary (30). Their children Mary (2) and Patrick (3 months) were younger than their visiting cousins. Annie would have visited with family, friends and neighbours. She would have noticed that there were two fewer households in Lippa. There would have been talk of the Congested

District's purchase of the Davy estate in Spiddal parish and the other efforts to secure land for tenants. *The Connacht Tribune* weekly papers for June 1911 reported a trade congress in Galway in June that addressed unemployment and the resultant emigration, the local elections for Galway District Councillors in Spiddal, the Oughterad Quarter Sessions report of a fortune dispute in an arranged marriage, and the welcoming address given by Father Farragher when the Irish Chief Secretary Augustine Birrell visited Aran. Annie's first mass at St Enda's would have been a proud moment for her.

Annie's favourite teacher Sister Gertrude Dooley was still teaching at the Presentation School, and Annie certainly would have looked forward to introducing little Mary Gertrude to her namesake; however, the child became fatally ill with diphtheria. Family tradition says she was exposed to the disease on the ship, but there were frequent outbreaks of diphtheria in Galway City and the surrounding countryside until immunization was introduced in 1931.[56] The little girl is buried with her grandparents in the graveyard in Cnoc. Her death was not recorded in the parish register. For the rest of her life, Annie felt that the child's death was a judgment. She had sacrificed her child to satisfy her own desire. On the other hand, she was favoured by Providence. Annie and young John were booked to return to America aboard the *Titanic*, but her father advised against it. 'It's a new ship, Annie, let someone else try it first'.

Neither Annie nor Jim ever returned to Ireland. They had five more children. Annie's daughter Eileen, a lively little girl in a loving family, remembers her father as a serious, loving man, a 'leg-puller', who loved poetry. While Annie was tall and slender, Jim was short and squarely built. His education was limited to the Kildrinagh National School; however, he knew Latin and algebra, and he figured out how to sink a well on the family farm before he emigrated. EIleen's memories of Annie are of her sweet nature, her gentle humour, her quiet industry. There was always a pot of tea for her half-dozen close friends who found a good listener, a wise counsellor who never lectured. Eileen, who entered religious life in her teens, describes the Phelans as a happy family and did not recall any of the pessimism that Annie expressed in the letters she wrote as a young woman.

Annie's youngest child Frank was born when she was in her mid-forties; the late child took its toll on her health. As a boy, Frank returned from school anxious till he found her at home or in her hillside garden, wearing her turn-of-the century hat, happiest when nurturing small creatures and tending her flowers. Her benediction was, 'May the Lord look sideways at it'. At the same time, Annie was no fool. She saved her Irish for an ironic '*Mar dhea go raibh*' to describe those letting on to be what they were not.[57]

She was fiercely loyal. She warmed to that quality in Mico, the Claddagh fisherman hero of her favourite book, Walter Macken's *Rain on the Wind* (1950). (Did she know that Macken had gone to the Presentation National School in Rahoon between 1918 and 1923?) Frank says the song 'Danny Boy' captures Annie with its nostalgic 'sunshine and shadow' and its expression of enduring human love, the fidelity she valued in herself and others (p. 55).

Both Annie and Jim were Catholics who found strength in their deep faith. She had a devotion to the rosary, and in her later years, when she seldom left home, she went out to mass and to First Fridays. Nothing suggests that Annie considered a vocation, but Jim had thought of joining the Irish Christian Brothers before he emigrated. As Annie gently but firmly led Jim to Pittsburgh and to a secure job on the streetcar, she steered some of her children to choose religious life.

The Irish women of Annie's generation were the founding mothers of the Irish Church in America. It was Irish and Irish-American religious who provided education, social and spiritual support to the immigrant Irish and their children. They represented Irish values and ethos in America. For Annie who believed that life was essentially tragic, her children's vocations would bring them safely through life in this world.

As Annie had packed her trunk for America, her daughters Kathleen and Eileen packed their trunks to enter the Sisters of St. Joseph while they were still schoolgirls.[58] Annie, Jim and the younger children spent Sunday afternoons visiting them in their convent parlours in the mining towns of western Pennsylvania. If the visit included a look into the sisters' schoolrooms, Jim would leave drawings of rabbits on the board to delight the children.

Later Frank picked up his bag and left home at 17 for the junior seminary at Notre Dame, the motherhouse of the Holy Cross Congregation. That Frank's vocation brought him to Notre Dame was especially meaningful to Annie, for she had developed a passion for Notre Dame football. She and Frank listened to the Fighting Irish on the radio, and while Annie ironed, Frank made a gridiron on the floor from straws. They figured that the line of scrimmage was somewhere between the twenty and thirty yard lines. For her, the Notre Dame–University of Pittsburgh game was a contest between the truth of the Virgin Mary and the agnosticism of Pitt in a country where her hero Al Smith couldn't be elected president and where Father Coughlin warned Catholic America about the threat of international bankers. Her John was a Notre Dame student, but her Frank became one of Notre Dame's own, a Holy Cross priest.

Frank was ordained in June 1954 when Annie was 75. She visited him in Washington when he was a seminarian. She travelled by train and delighted her companions by announcing to the conductor that she was on her way to Washington to get one of those mink coats![59] The Easter before Frank's ordination she came bringing the *panniculi* for his priest's hands that she herself embroidered with a Celtic motif. Frank asked for her wedding ring to incorporate into the design of his ordination chalice.[60] It symbolised her vocation as a mother of Holy Cross religious as well as his own vocation as a priest. Writing of his request for the ring in 'Lonely House Now', Frank described how the Celtic cross formed by Annie's ring fused his parents through his chalice bringing the greatest possible blessing.

In his autobiographical novel *Four Ways of Computing Midnight*, Frank describes anointing her when she died at eighty on 4 July 1959:

> I wanted to make sure of one thing: that she died as she had lived, with her deep faith intact, so that Despair, black Despair, would not creep in at the final moment between herself and that final brightness which she and all our people believe in from the beginning. [61]

Assisted by the men of her class, Frank was the chief celebrant at Annie's Solemn High Mass of Requiem. A classmate's remark anticipated the ecclesiastical changes that would come with Vatican 2. 'You know, Father, through it all I had the feeling we were burying more than your mother; I had the feeling we were burying Holy Mother Church herself'.[62]

Jim was despondent. 'Tis a lonely house now', he groaned when he returned home after Annie's funeral. He survived her by two years. As they had treasured photographs of each other, Jim asked Frank if he could paint Annie. Frank said he couldn't, but Jim had a portrait of Annie tied in a bundle in his trunk: her letters. She had disparaged them and asked Jim to destroy them, but he preserved every one (p. 64). She had spent her life with the refrain, 'Let something remain'. Her letters are her legacy.

## Notes to Introduction

1   'Statistical review of immigration 1820–1910', *Abstracts of the Reports of the Immigration Commission* I (Washington, 1911), p. 92.

2   St Éanna's parish records indicate that Annie was born in 1879; however, in the United States 1900 census, she reports her date of birth as 1880. A child was usually baptized the third day after its birth, but there was often a delay before the birth was reported. Sometimes the registration date was given as the date of birth. Conversation with Rahoon Parish and Presentation Convent archivist Sr Máire Mac Niallais, 19 Jan. 2003.

The Irish word *liopa* means a lip or a seal's flipper. A local history says the precise meaning of the placename is unknown and that the townland is a long narrow finger of land that stretches two miles north into the bog and mountain. In 1901, there were twelve houses in Lippa; in 1911, there were ten houses. By 1982, the number had fallen to six houses. Tom Kenny (ed.), *Bearna agus na Forbacha: A Local History* (Bearna, 1982).

The name of the village of Spiddal comes from the Irish word *óspidéal*. There was a temporary fever hospital in Spiddal in 1817; in 1847, during the Great Irish Famine, the local fever hospital was in Spiddal. James P. Murray, *Galway: A Medico-Social History* (Galway, 1994), p 76. A watercolour from the sketchbook of Louise Catherine Beaufort (1781–1863), now at Trinity College, Dublin (MS 8269), shows the famine orphan refuge at Spiddal.

3   James Murray, 'Lesser-known famine in Galway', *Galway Roots*, IV (1996), pp. 83–97.

4   Patrick O'Donnell married Margaret Concannon of the townland of Leanarievagh (Léana Riabhach) on 27 September 1860. Their witnesses were Pat O'Donnell and Bridget Concannon. The groom's £2 for the ceremony was considerably more than any other man paid to get married in the parish in the autumn of 1860. I am indebted to Galway Presentation Convent and Rahoon parish archivist Sr Máire Mac Niallais for this information from the Rahoon Parish records.

5   In 1900, there were 243,000 immigrants in the area. Marisol Bello, 'Industrial heyday marks peak of influx', *Pittsburgh Tribune-Review*, 24 Sept. 2002.

6   Oh, I pity the mother who rears up the child,
      And likewise the father who labours and toils,
      To try to support them, he works night and day,
      And when they are reared up, they go away.

This is a stanza from the traditional emigration ballad 'Thousands are Sailing'. In O'Flaherty's story, 'Going into Exile', Patrick Feeney says to his emigrating son, 'I was thinking of that potato field you sowed alone last spring the time I had the influenza. I never set eyes on that man could do it better. It's a cruel world that takes you away from the land that God made you for.' 'Going into exile', in Maureen Murphy and James MacKillop (eds), *Irish Literature: A Reader* (Syracuse, 1987), p. 280.

7   Maud Wynne, *An Irishman and His Family: Lord Morris and Killanin*. (London, 1937), p. 34. Lord Killanin's house was destroyed in 1922; it was partially rebuilt. Lord Killanin and Michael V. Duignan, *The Shell Guide to Ireland* (London, 1967), p. 429.

8   John Millington Synge, 'From Galway to Gorumna', in Alan Price (ed.), *The Collected Works of J. M. Synge: Prose* (London, 1966), p. 286.

9   Stephen Gwynn, *A Holiday in Connemara* (London, 1909), pp. 51, 52.

10   Frank Phelan, 'Lonely House Now', *Four Ways of Computing Midnight* (New York, 1985), p. 158. The Silver Strand, An Trá Geal, is just east of the townland of Léana Riabhach, the home of Annie's mother's people.

11   Domhnall Ó Duibhne (Daniel Deeney), the Spiddal schoolmaster published *Peasant Lore from Gaelic Ireland* in 1900. Lady Gregory had Irish lessons with Ó Duibhne when she visited the Morrises in 1897. She says she encouraged Ó Duibhne to collect folklore, and she offered a prize for stories. *Seventy Years, 1852–1922* (Gerrards Cross, 1974) pp. 318–19. The site of the original national school is the present Teach an tSagairt. The girls' school was across the street on the site of the present library.

12   Index to the Register of Rahoon Convent National School, p. 35. Annie is no. 4082.

13   When Nora left school in April 1896 at the age of twelve, the Sisters of Mercy found her a job as a portress at the Presentation convent in Rahoon. Brenda Maddox, *Nora: The Real Life of Molly Bloom* (Boston, 1988), p. 13.

14   Margaret C. Scully, 'A study of the emergence and growth of the provision of education for children in Galway City since 1800', unpublished thesis, University College Cork, p. 166. Annie's contemporary, the Indreabhán writer Micheál Breathnach (1881–1908), served as a monitor as part of his training as a national schoolteacher before he went to work for the London branch of the Gaelic League in 1901. Later, Máirtín Ó Cadhain (1906–1970) was monitor in the Spiddal National School.

15   The 4 Jan. 1899 issue of *An Claidheamh Soluis* mentions that pupils from the Presentation School presented a programme of Irish songs and recitations to the Galway Gaelic League.

16   Liam O'Flaherty, *Skerritt* (New York, 1932), p. 11.

17   I am grateful to Mary E. Daly, Margaret MacCurtain, Sr Máire Mac Niallais and Máirtín Ó Flathartaigh for information about the importance of music in the national school curriculum.

18   Máirtín Ó Cadhain, 'The year 1912', *The Road to Bright City*, trans. Eoghan Ó Tuairisc (Dublin, 1981).

19   Maureen Murphy, 'The Fionnuala factor: Irish sibling migration at the turn of the century', in Anthony Bradley and Maryann Gialanella Valiulis (eds), *Gender and Sexuality in Modern Ireland* (Amherst, 1997), p. 93.

20   N. R. P. Bonsor, '*Adria* 1896/*Narva* 1905/*Khazan* 1906', *North Atlantic Seaway*, I (Newton Abbot, 1975), p. 402. Paul Loudon-Brown. *The White Star Line: An Illustrated History: 1870–1930* (Norfolk, 1991), pp. 21, 137.

21 See p. 64. Jim's widowed mother sent a telegram to the police at Queenstown. The Royal Irish Constabulary officer who blocked Jim's passage up the gangplank to the tender said to Jim that he had to listen to the summons, but he didn't have to follow its instructions. Interview with Frank Phelan, 14 Nov. 2002.

22 List or Manifest of Alien Immigrants for the *Adria* sailing from Queenstown, 27 October 1898. Arrived in Philadelphia 10 November.

23 Bridget left Ireland in 1888; Mary followed two years later. The Lydons lived with or next door to the Keadys on Liberty Street when Annie arrived. According to Eileen Phelan (Sr M. Gabriel), they moved to Epiphany Street and later up to the hill district. Conversation, 2 Mar. 2003. The 1910 census indicates that the two families moved to the Third Ward where the Lydons and the Keadys occupied the same premises at 110 Elm Street. Frank Phelan says that the Lydons and the Keadys were always mentioned as a single unit. Interview, 9 Apr. 2004.

24 See pp. 37, 39, 43–4, 51,76–7, 83.

25 See pp. 40, 48, 63–4, 71, 73, 83, 87.

26 See pp. 64, 66, 67, 69, 74, 77, 84, 85, 93, 101, 140.

27 Colonel James Martinu Schoonmaker (1842–1927), commander of the 14th Pennsylvania Cavalry, was the youngest colonel in the Union Army. For his bravery leading a cavalry charge at the Battle of Star Fort, Virginia, he was awarded the Medal of Honor in 1899. (The date coincides with Annie's employment.) His business interests included iron, coke and the Pittsburgh and Lake Erie Railroad. Tom and Nancy McAdams, 'Colonel James Martinu Schoonmaker–Civil War Medal of Honor', tandnmca/civilwar/schoonmaker.html.

28 Gabriel P. Weisberg, 'From Paris to Pittsburgh: visual culture and American taste, 1880–1910', *Collecting in the Gilded Age: Art Patronage in Pittsburgh, 1890–1910* (Pittsburgh, 1997), p. 201.

29 Scottish-born Mary 'May' Taylor Mellon (1872–1942) came to the United States in 1894. In 1896, she married William Larimer Mellon (1868–1949), the son of James Ross Mellon and Rachel Larimer Mellon and the nephew of Andrew Mellon. W. L. made his own fortune when he founded, with other Pittsburgh businessmen, the Gulf Oil Corporation in January 1907.

30 The two older Mellon children had connections with Ireland in their adult years. Matthew Taylor Mellon was the patron of the Ulster American Folk Park at Camphill near the homestead from which Thomas Mellon emigrated to the United States with his parents. Rachel Larimer Mellon, who was named after her paternal grandmother, married John Walton, Jr, in 1922; her son-in-law, Walter Curley, was Ambassador to Ireland. The editor spoke with Mrs. Walton on the phone; she remembered Annie as a nice presence in her early life. A Pittsburgh philanthropist, Mrs Walton celebrated her 100th birthday on 16 February 1999.

31 Information from the United States Census for 1900. *Twelfth Census of the United States.* Schedule. No.1 – Population. Microfilm Roll 351. M454.

32 See pp. 37, 39, 44, 49, 55, 63–4, 65, 70, 72.

33 Conversation with Frank Phelan, 14 Nov. 2002.

34 Barry Paris, '*Song of Haiti*: the lives of Dr Larimer and Gwen Mellon', *Pittsburgh Post-Gazette*, 17 Sept. 2000.

35 See pp. 49, 50, 54, 70.

36 Ethel Spencer, *The Spencers of Amberson Avenue: A Turn-of-the-Century Memoir* (Pittsburgh, 1983), p. 75.

37 Matthew Mellon's privately printed *Watermellons* (1974) describes his childhood. Burton Hersh, *The Mellon Family: A Fortune in History* (New York, 1978), p. 182.

38 See pp. 46, 54, 70, 85.

39 See pp. 37, 39, 42, 45, 47–8, 49, 56, 61–2, 64, 66, 90, 93, 96–7.

40 Ó Cadhain, 'The Year 1912', *The Road to Bright City*, trans. Eoghan O Tuarisc (Dublin, 1981), p. 36.

41 Eilís Dillon, *The Bitter Glass* (London, 1958), p. 144. Dillon lived with her family at Bearna Pier, near Léana Riabhach, in 1926.

42 David E. Koskoff, *The Mellons: The Chronicle of America's Richest Family* (New York, 1978), p. 127.

43 Conversation with Frank Phelan, 14 Nov. 2002. George Eastman invented the box camera in 1888; roll film followed in 1891. Was it Annie's influence that turned Matthew Mellon into a keen photographer who photographed his Grand Tour (1914) with an old Kodak camera? Burton Hersh, *The Mellon Family: A Fortune in History* (New York, 1978), p. 185.

44 See pp. 48, 52, 60, 62, 64.

45 W. L. Mellon was involved with the growth and expansion of the electric streetcar service in Pittsburgh in the 1890s. 'Long before he got himself into the street rail business, W. L. Mellon owned the basic rights of way'. Hersh, *Mellon Family*, p. 448.

46 Annie may have been referring to Fire Engine No. 14, Truck D which was located on Neville Street next to Duquesne Garden; however, the fire station does not appear to be on the route to either Shadyside Academy or the Alinda School.

47 Lord Killanin, *St Enda's* (Spiddal, 1950),

48 Maureen Murphy, 'The Fionnuala factor: Irish sibling migration at the turn of the century', in Anthony Bradley and Maryann Gialanella Valiulis (eds), *Gender and Sexualilty in Modern Ireland* (Amherst, 1997), p. 93.

49 W. L. Mellon's trips to to Beaumont, Texas in August 1902 laid the groundwork for the company that became Gulf Oil.

50 The Church of the Epiphany in the Lower Hill section of Pittsburgh was dedicated on 20August 1903. It was the pro-cathedral and residence of Bishop Phelan until the new

cathedral was completed in 1906. Msgr Francis Glenn. *Shepherds of the Faith 1843–1993: A Brief History of the Bishops of the Catholic Diocese of Pittsburgh* (Pittsburgh, 1993), p. 120.

51 Phelan, 'The breaking of the string', *Four Ways of Computing Midnight* (New York, 1985), p. 9.

52 Msgr Francis Glenn, *Shepherds of the Faith 1843–1993: A Brief History of the Bishops of the Catholic Diocese of Pittsburgh* (Pittsburgh, 1993), p. 56.

53 Hasia Diner, *Erin's Daughters in America* (Baltimore, 1983), p. 54.

54 Conversation with Frank Phelan, 14 Nov. 2002. Annie refers to the series of Edward Harrigan and Tony Hart's plays about the Irish in the tenements of New York's Lower East Side.

55 Sister M. Gertrude Dooley's obituary in the Presentation Archives describes the qualities that endeared her to Annie. 'In her day she was regarded as a great school nun both for her talent in imparting knowledge and in keeping up perfect discipline among her pupils. She had charge of the senior school for many years which she brought to a high degree of efficiency. She took a deep interest in preparing the poor girls for their future life and they keenly appreciated her efforts especially in their after lives when from America and elsewhere they often wrote to her and reminded her of the good teaching and training she gave them and to which they attributed much of their success in life.' Death of Sr M. Gertrude Dooley, 1924. Archives of the Presentation Convent, Rahoon, County Galway. I am grateful to Sister Máire Mac Niallais for this information.

56 James Murray, 'Lesser known famine in Galway', *Galway Roots* IV (1906), pp. 138, 149.

57 Conversation with Frank Phelan, 14 Nov. 2002.

58 Kathleen (Sister M. Caroline) received permission to enter the junior novitiate of the Sisters of St Joseph at the age of 13. Eileen followed when she was 18. The Sisters of St Joseph are a French order that was founded in Le Puy, France. Six St. Joseph sisters arrived at Carondelet, Missouri in 1836 to teach the deaf and to work with native Americans. The Phelan sisters' congregation is now part of the United States Federation of the Sisters of St Joseph.

59 Annie was referring to the vicuna coat scandal that resulted in the 1958 resignation of President Eisenhower's Chief of Staff, Sherman Adams (1899–1986), for accepting a fur coat from New England industrialist Bernard Goldfine. Phelan. 'Lonely house now', *Four Ways*, p. 157.

60 Ibid., pp. 159, 192.

61 Ibid. p. 192.

62 Ibid. p. 195.

ANNIE O'DONNELL
*to*
JAMES P. PHELAN

✦

# *1901*

✦

Spring Lake
New Jersey
August 2nd, 1901

Dear Jim:

Your letter which I received only this morning more than surprised me. I thought you certainly had forgotten me by this time. You are the only one I heard from of all I met on the *Adria*. Like yourself, when I got into Pittsburgh, other things seemed to bother me, so that I gave up all hopes of either hearing from or writing to anybody.

To start with, I did not like the Smoky city and loneliness nearly broke my *poor heart*. When Xmas time came, I longed for my Ma's presence, but I was too far away. Once I started to work, things were coming much easier. I got an easy place for seven months, and then changed for another, even nicer, position which I am holding just now. I have travelled a good deal with them and am now spending the summer in Spring Lake, a seaside resort.[1]

Your letter was forwarded to me by my sister. She must have kept it quite a while before forwarding it. I should very much like to know if you have yet learned to like Uncle Sam.[2] I am sure I don't and never will like it as well as dear old Galway. I hear from home quite often. My friends there are still true.

You must write very soon again and tell me all about yourself. Forgive me if I say that I barely remember your face. In fact I must say that I have but the slightest idea of what you looked like.

When I got off in Pittsburgh on that day we parted, I didn't thank you for your kindness to me on board the *Adria*. Now as this is one of my busy days, I must bring my letter to a finish and will give you my present address as well as my Pittsburgh one. I am a child's maid so am almost always travelling about, but either one of these addresses will find me.

Hoping to hear from you very soon. I remain, Annie O'Donnell

Annie O'Donnell
c/o W. L. Mellon
Box 249 Spring Lake
New Jersey

Annie O'Donnell
c/o W. L. Mellon
4616 Bayard Street–E. End
Pittsburgh, Pa.

1   Spring Lake, a Victorian seaside resort on New Jersey shore, takes its name from the underground springs that feed the lake.
2   Annie's reference to her loyalty to Uncle Sam expresses some of the ambivalence Irish immigrants felt about America.

-------

13 AUGUST 1901

Spring Lake, N.J.
August 13th 1901

Dear Jim,
I am awfully glad to see by your last letter that you are happy and that you have your sister with you.[1]

I can imagine how lonely you must have felt before she came, for I assure you it is anything but pleasant to be a stranger in a strange land knowing little or nothing of its customs. But Jim, friends are not always the ones who help you along, and if you take notice, this is the very country they help you least in. I very soon found that out, for I was only a few days in Pittsburgh when I became as independent as U. Sam himself even if I didn't have one dollar to my name. Still I held my head up, became very reserved and kept my own affairs to myself and for a time was considered very proud but finally came out all right, so that today, I can take my place with the very best of them. People think all the more of me because I am reserved and don't pick up with everybody that comes along.

I am very poor for making friends but those I do make are very *sincere*. I have met one such friend. She is working with me, and in fact has been in this family for years.[2] We have travelled together and she has almost taken the place of mother to me. I wish you could see her Jim, for I know you would like her as I certainly do. I told her about you and how, after almost three years, you wrote your first letter when I had almost forgotten you.

If we ever have a chance of going anyway near your place, we will certainly try to see you, but I don't think there is any such luck. Still we go every winter to Florida, and who knows but we would stop off there on our way. Well, let us hope that way any how.

My last recollection of you, and it was a jolly one, was when you were coming along the deck with the tea things and holding on for dear life to the rope!! But never mind if we don't meet here. Perhaps we would on another *Adria*. I still hold on to that little cross. My vaccination turned out all right after giving me a painful arm for a few weeks.

I had my pictures taken about eighteen months ago, haven't any with me but will send you one when I get home to Pittsburgh which will not be before the end of September. This is such a quiet place. I will be glad when we get home. There is nothing in the line of enjoyment for us except surf bathing and bicycling in which I take great delight especially in cycling. I learned to ride here two years ago.

Isn't this summer a scorcher? My! but it was hot in Pittsburgh, but here it is perfectly lovely. We are only a square from the ocean and enjoy its breezes to the full extent.[3] Well, Jim, I think now that I have told all the nonsense I could glean. I must finish hoping to hear from you very soon again. And remain as ever, Annie

1   Jim persuaded his sister Helena (Lena) Phelan (1880–1966) to emigrate to Indianapolis in December 1899. She later moved to Iowa (see p. 76–7) and married Warren McMillan, a railroadman in Burlington, Iowa. Family genealogical notes made by Eileen Phelan (Sr M. Gabriel).
2   Annie's friend Ellen Comphreys emigrated from England in 1895; she probably joined the Mellon household in 1897 when Matthew was born.
3   Annie is probably referring to Hastings Square between First and Ocean Avenues.

---

25 AUGUST 1901

Spring Lake, N.J.
August 25th, 1901

Dear Jim,

Our time in Spring L. is coming to an end sooner than we expected as our folks have now decided to spend a few weeks at the mountains before going home. I am rather sorry as I like the ocean and the seashore in general much better than any other place. But still it will be a change for us, as a person naturally gets tired of the same thing. Spring L. is a very quiet place and to a certain extent monotonous. Not very much to divert the attention, but for nature's admirers, I hardly think there is any other place that supplies more food for both thought and admiration, and for those wishing to spend a few months quietly, it is second to none.

There are lakes, rivers etc. in the vicinity, just beautiful with lots of fishing and rowing, but to me none will ever be dearer than that beautiful *ocean*. I love to sit on the sands and listen to the roar of its waters. Yes, it sounds far sweeter than the sweetest music while again it recalls but too well the memories of by gone days. Alas! days never to return. It alone can only tell of the many happy days I spent by its waters in dear old Galway, and for one such day, I would now give almost anything.

They were the days when my heart was light and happy, and it was there also I slept and dreamt that *life* was beauty and from that sleep I woke and found in America that *life* was *duty*. Fate is cruel to some at least it was so to me, for when it placed the Atlantic between me and those I loved, it stamped a mark on my life never to be forgotten. What good does anything afford you when you have a dear Mother that you cannot see? Jim, do you mind that night when you told us of your leaving home, how I cried, yes, fit to break my heart, for I know then, as I do now, what parting with a Mother meant.[1]

That same night we expected a storm. We all felt kind of down-hearted, but consoled ourselves with the thought that the nearest and dearest must part. Well, I think I have said enough about sad things tonight, but it seems to me all my letters now-a-days are sad.

I wish your sister had stopped off at Pittsburgh for you know I would be very glad to see her.

Ellen, my friend that I wrote you of, is not Irish but comes from Chester, England, a catholic and a nice sensible woman about ten years older than I.[2] You know, Jim, I wouldn't give her for all the Irish girls I have ever met. She has been in this country for years and now talks of going back. I hate to think of that, for when she goes, I will lose a dear friend and one that has always taken a deep interest in all my doings so that with perfect confidence I can tell her anything I please.

Well, Jim, my picture I certainly will send as soon as possible, but I may have to get some taken as I am not sure whether I have any left or not, but I wish you would not wait for me to send mine as I would like to have yours very much.

Now I hope you will excuse this hasty note, Jim, and write me very soon again as we expect to leave here about the eleventh of next month, and I would like to have an answer before leaving, so now with kindest regards to all I remain as ever, Annie

1    Annie's recollection of weeping at Jim's description of leaving his mother is at odds with the family story that he ran away while his widowed mother was at mass. Conversation with Frank Phelan, 14 Nov. 2002.
2    Annie says that Ellen is not Irish; however, she was born in England of Irish parents. *Twelfth Census of the United States.* Schedule. No. 1 – Population. Microfilm Roll 351, M 454.

---

4 SEPTEMBER 1901

4th September, 1901
New York, N.Y.

c/o W. L. Mellon
4616 Bayard St. E. E.
Pittsburgh, Pa

Dear Jim,
I am alone and lonely tonight in the crowded city of New York. Mrs. Mellon and I are here on a shopping tour, but will return later in the week to Spring Lake to bid our final farewells to that delightful and (to me) eventful region. Well, Jim, I could see by your last letter that I must have made you feet quite hurt. Now I am awfully sorry, for as Ellen told me, I should not have recalled bitter memories. It is for one reason that I put on paper exactly the thing which comes foremost at the time of writing that I have come to almost hate it. When I read your letter, I felt a pang and would have undone that which I did if it were only possible. Of course I must say that I never look at the bright side of things notwithstanding the many times I have been told it.

You told me to remember you as the *Lad*. No, Jim, I will remember you as a kind friend who helped me along when I needed help most. I am one of these that never give up the old for the new. If you do a kind turn for me once, I shall never forget it.

Last week was quite a lovely one at Spring L. We had the Irish Rifle Association who came with Sir T. Lipton to compete with the American.[1] My! but it was nice to see them, and to think they were directly from our dear Isle. They did fine, beat the Americans at the first contest. The shooting takes place on the camping grounds, an extensive place especially for the soldiers during the months of July and August where they drill.[2]

Now it is quite late and am feeling tired after my trip as you can see by this scribble. I will close hoping to hear from you very soon and write one addressed to Pittsburgh. It will be forwarded to me. I don't know the Mountain address yet. With my *very kindest regards* to you, Jim. I remain as before, Annie

1   Competition between international rifle teams was popular in the nineteenth century. *Harper's Weekly*, 10 Oct. 1874, reported the excitement generated by the International Rifle Match between American and Irish rifle teams held at Creedmoor, Long Island on 16 September.

2   Annie is probably describing the National Guard training centre located on Sea Girt Avenue in Sea Girt, New Jersey, a town about two miles south of Spring Lake.

---

27 SEPTEMBER 1901

Pittsburgh [Pa.]
Sept. 27

My dear Jim,

I am back once more in the Smoky City, it is quite a change from our pleasant seaside and mountain resorts. Well, a word or so about our time at the Mountains. It was something great. I never had such a time in my life. Many a time I wished you were with us, for I know how you would enjoy it. We went to dances and hay rides and lots of parties, and everybody tried to show us a good time. We wished we could have stayed there much longer.

Do you remember those beautiful mountains we came through on our way here some distance from Pittsburgh. I think you mentioned them in one of your letters. Well, we were situated in the heart of them. The scenery was something which I cannot describe, for it was perfect!

Well, Jim, that long promised face of mine I am sending. It is not much, but it will remind you that you saw it once, and I do hope you will send me yours for even if you are in Indiana, I hold a spot in my heart for you. I wish you had pitched your tent in Pittsburgh instead of going so far, but still we must put up with these things, for as I said once before, the nearest and dearest must part. We may meet again and perhaps have a dance like that one of Mayo Jim's. What about Galway Jim?[1] He was a pretty nice fellow. I liked him so well. Is it not funny to see us all so widely scattered and no one left to tell the tale, as it were, only you and I.

I wish you had told me of your New York friends for I could have made time to see them, and you know I spent 3 months of last year in New York and 2 weeks in Brooklyn.[2] I have visited both places several times since I came to live with the Mellons.

By the way are you going to the Expo?[3] Our folks are going, but I am not. They are leaving the children with Ellen and I. I hope you will excuse this hurried letter as we have been quite busy since we came home. Your last letter, Jim, I didn't get for a week after its arrival in Pittsburgh. Do write soon again and a *long* letter.

I expect to go out on Sunday to see some of my friends and acquaintances. Remember me to your sister and friends. I have been once on a streetcar since we came home. It was rather a treat. Well, dear Jim, it is almost eleven and quite time to retire, so I will bid you good night and with love I remain as ever Annie.

Write very soon.

1    Mayo Jim was Jim Murray; Galway Jim was Jim Butler. List or Manifest of Alien Immigrants for the *Adria* sailing from Queenstown, 27 Oct. 1898.

2    Jim had cousins in Brooklyn. See pp. 46, 52, 60, 62, 64.

3    The Mellons visited the Pan-American Exposition at Buffalo, New York the month after President William McKinley was assassinated on 6 September by the anarchist Leon Czolgosz. The Exposition ran from 1 May to 2 November 1901.

---

## 18 OCTOBER 1901

Pittsburgh Pa.
Oct 18th 1901

My dear Jim,

It is almost time that I should answer your letter, I know you will think me very neglectful for not answering much sooner which I intended doing, but I assure you I have been quite busy and the little spare time I get which is usually at night I give to sewing. Since our folks went to Buffalo and left us with the children, you know we feel a big responsibility.

You seem to think your letters in the past were not very acceptable, but that is not so, for I would never have answered them if I had thought that. It is very hard to please me in letters I do know, but must say yours are too interesting to leave unanswered even if it takes me a long time to do so. It is not through lack of thought, for if I did not care for a person, I would never condescend to put my thoughts on paper.

Life seems just the same old way here. I have been out just twice since, had a pretty good time. Everybody seemed glad to see me back. Spent one Sunday with my sisters who wanted to know all about the Indiana letter they got for me. We talked a good deal of you. They live opposite the Union Station where we parted that day pretty near three years ago. There is a new depot built there now, yes, one of the finest I have seen in my travels.[1]

I have two sisters here, both married long before I dreamt of leaving home. One, the eldest of our whole family, has two little girls and a boy and the other has a boy and girl.[2] I was but a mere child when they left for America. Neither of us knew the other when we met. I am the baby girl of the family. There is only one boy younger and he is the real baby although he is about sixteen.[3] We had in our home originally five girls and two boys, but they are almost all far apart now.[4] All my sisters being married but one. Father and mother still living. I hear from them quite often.

I was born in a little place called Spiddal about twenty miles from Galway City. My parents always wished me to be a school teacher, so at the age of thirteen, they sent me to the Convent of the Presentation (Galway) where I was appointed monitor which position I held till October of '98.[5] I did not board at the Convent but simply went there to school, and it is there that those dear happy days I told you of were spent.[6]

When I left there, I made my debut in this world and not until I reached Pittsburgh did I know of that selfish deceit etc. that rule this world. It was then that I missed everything, for I was thrown entirely on my own resources. And it was there also I chose my friends (very few), became independent and reserved and have been so ever since. When I met Ellen, I met with the one I often wished for. She is dignified and won't associate with everyone, and she is one of the three in my whole life that won my entire affection, a thing which is rather difficult to do, but once done is done forever.

In the winter of '98 I weighed 116 pounds. A year later 127, later still 137½ then came down to 120, but I have grown quite tall since you saw me, my height being somewhere round 5' 6" or perhaps a little more.[7]

Well now, Jim, I think I have told you most every little thing of interest, so you will please excuse me for my mistakes as am in quite a hurry as usual, and hope you will write me *very soon*. I suppose I don't need to tell you to remember me to anybody. I get my share of teasing here about the little print letters from Indianapolis, but I never mind. I am always glad to get them and do write a long one very soon.

Will now close with love x.

from Annie

1    The new Union Station designed by Daniel H. Burnham was built between 1898 and 1903. In his story 'Luxuria Larvata', Frank Phelan mentions old St Patrick's Church, built at the corner of Liberty and Washington Streets, near the freight yards of the Union depot.
2    Both sisters appear in the 1884 parish census when Bridget was 19 and Mary was 13. Bridget left home in 1888; Mary followed in 1890. Bridget married a Lydon and Mary a Keady; both are local names. Bridget was listed as age 47 in the 1910 census; Mary was 40.
3    John went briefly to the United States in 1902. He is listed in the 1901 Census as the 15-year-old son of farmer Patrick O'Donnell.
4    In the 1901 Census, Patrick (34) and Margaret (23) were also listed in the Lippa homestead. By 1911, only Patrick and Annie's older sisters Honor (Nora) and Margaret lived in Ireland. Nora married Michael Griffin of Newtown, Moycullen, County Galway; Margaret married James Faherty of Allia, Inverin, County Galway.
5    The records of the Presentation School in Rahoon indicate that Annie entered the school at the age of 16 from the National School in Spiddal. She spent two years there doing the monitor course. School records indicate that she left the school on 16 April 1898.
6    Annie probably stayed with her mother's people who lived in the townland of Léana Riabhach located just west of An Trá Gheal, the Silver Strand.
7    Annie's account of her growth in height and weight is, of course, a measure of the good life in America. When she tells Jim he's gotten stout (see pp. 48, 64), she means it as a compliment.

———

5? NOVEMBER 1901

New York
Tuesday night

My dear Jim,

I have been waiting patiently since I got your last letter for your picture which however has not yet arrived. I left strict orders for my mail to be forwarded before leaving Pittsburgh on Friday last.

We are all here on a visit of four weeks at the same place where we spent three months of last year. We are on the West Side quite a long way from the large downtown stores. Yes, more than an hour's ride. We have not as yet seen anything beyond the ordinary but are planning to get a day off soon to see the stores. Last year we had but two children to care for but this time we have one extra, so that is harder to get away from them.[1]

I am just trying my very hardest to get an opportunity of seeing your cousins now that I am here, but Brooklyn is such a way from here I don't know if I can. Anyhow, Jim, even if I am inconvenienced, I will do my utmost to see them. When I can not see *you*, the very least I may do is to see some one belonging to you.

Well Jim, how did you ever get that nice poetry you sent me?[2] I am sure if you had it made to order, you could not have suited my case better. It was the most appropriate piece I ever got. Those few pieces I sent you with the magazine (which I hope you received all right) were written for me by a dear friend some nights before meeting you. The marked story I wanted you to read. I get the magazines monthly since I came to live with Ellen. Let me know if you are fond of reading, Jim, and what is your favourite kind?

We had a very pleasant Hallow eve playing several tricks. Do you mind the Hallow eve we spent together, it looked like any other didn't it?[3] We did not even have apples. Still, we appeared happy, but you see riches don't make happiness.

Well, Jim, do write soon and in the mean time, I hope your picture will come as I am most anxious to see if I can even then form an idea of that boy who was the life of the *Adria*. It seems too bad that *time* has such an effect on memory as well as on several other things. If we had but a small part of that great factor of past time given us, what we would have done and undone? W*e ourselves* only can tell.

It is now getting quite late so I must finish and ask you once again to write me very soon to the enclosed address [4] And I now remain as ever

    with love, Annie

P.S. Be sure and *remember* me to all,

1    Margaret Mellon was born in 1901.
2    Irish National School education featured poetry that students memorized. Frank Phelan describes his father writing poetry in 'The Breaking of the String', p. 9.
3    Annie and Jim spent Halloween, 1898, on the *Adria*.
4    The address given was c/o Mrs. Lederle, 471 West 143rd Street, New York. Mrs Lederle, May Mellon's sister, was married to the chemist Ernst J. Lederle (1865–1921), founder of the Lederle Laboratories and Antitoxin Laboratories. He served two terms as New York City's Health Commissioner (1902–4, 1910–14). His second terms began with the notorious Typhoid Mary case. He released her, found her work as a laundress and ordered her never to work again as a cook. The Lederles were close to the Mellons. They named their daughter Mary Taylor Lederle after May. The Lederle home was located in Hamilton Heights, an area north of 125th Street. The present no. 471 house is on West 143rd Street between Convent and Amsterdam Avenues.

---

12 DECEMBER 1901

        [Pittsburgh, Pa.]
        Thursday night
        Dec. 12th

My dear Jim,
That long looked for letter and picture arrived *at last*. How I thought you were never going to answer my note. Still, I maintained to the last that there was something beyond the ordinary which might have interfered with your writing.

I am sorry you have not been well, but you try and keep warm, for you have not the warmest place on earth right now in weather below zero. I often think of you standing in those cars pretty near frozen.

I can not proceed any further without making some comments on your picture. It almost took me a day to say whether you looked like the Jim I used to know or not. Finally I came to the conclusion that there were some points of resemblance.

If you had it taken bust and without the hat, I could see more plainly, but as it is, I can see you in a sort of a hazy, indistinct way, of course allowing for *Time* to make some changes which it is bound to do. You have gotten very stout I should think, and you look so youthful. Those that have seen it say you look like a mere boy, but I know different. Anyhow, you look pretty nice.

Well we got home, just two days before your letter came, from New York. Were glad to get back again to the Smoky City, as we did not have much of a time in N. York. I know you will think me queer for not seeing your cousins after your sister going to the trouble of writing, but I assure you I made every effort but in vain. The only time I could call my own was from 2 till 6 one afternoon. There is nothing which would have afforded me more pleasure whilst there than to see them if possible, but you know I am always rather unfortunate in matters of that kind. I have never known myself yet to try anything without having a certain amount of disappointment in connection with it. Of course that's nothing new. It has been my luck so far through life.

Well, Jim, I am glad you read a good deal, for it is an elegant thing. I only wish I could devote more time to it than I do. If you ever come in contact with two books called the *The Crisis* and *Granstark*, or *The Story of a Love Behind a Throne* you read them, for they are fine.[1] You have a good joke on me about those pieces of poetry. I didn't know that you saw them with me.

Well, now it is almost too late to say any more, but I have to remind you once more that I am quite pleased with your picture and thank you very much for sending it. I only wish it were the original, and many a tale of the old *Adria* would be told and retold.

However, let us hope that some day we will meet and *then* we can see which one *Time* has favoured most.

Now Good Night and with
love I remain same old Annie.

x

Excuse all those mispelled words.

---

1  The American novelist Winston Churchill (1871–1927) was a widely read author at the turn of the twentieth century. He wrote the American Civil War romance, *The Crisis*, in 1901. George Barr McCutheon's *Granstark: The Story of a Love Behind a Throne* (1901), a romantic escape novel set in a fictitious European country, was an American bestseller. There were silent and sound film versions of the book made in 1915 and 1925.

---

23 DECEMBER 1901

[Pittsburgh, Pa.]
Monday Dec. 23rd, 1901

My dear Jim,

On Saturday last your nice gift reached me, and I must say it was most acceptable.[1] You are still the same kind thoughtful fellow that I knew some time ago. Ellen was almost was as pleased as if she herself got it. You know she is my dearest friend, and I will not be wrong in saying that she loves me more than anyone else outside Mother, and there is nothing that pleases her more than to see me happy.

We often sit in our room and talk of you, and since your picture has taken a prominent place on my table, we never miss a day that we don't talk of you. Of course I come in for my share of teasing, but it takes no effect as I can stand quite a little bit of it. Ellen has a soft spot for you and expressed a great desire of seeing you when I read your letter to her. As you say, we are not *so very far* apart, and you know there is *one* here who would give anything to see you, so let us hope that one day you will condescend to visit our

Smoky City. Of course I shall leave that for you to decide. You know best.

I promise you to wait patiently for your picture, but I hate to see you bothering so much trying to suit such a fastidious creature.

From all appearances today, we will have a green Xmas. It is not too bad. We are planning very hard here trying to get to early Mass on Xmas morning as it is quite hard to get away from the children. We both sleep with them.

Our lady is treating us to tickets for the Theatre to see 'Ben Hur'[2] the night after Christmas, (I wish you were with us; how different it would be.)

Now Jim, I must finish as we are very busy preparing for 'Santa Claus'.

So with loving and best wishes
for all I remain
Annie

*Write Soon*

1    Jim apparently sent Annie a pin or a brooch. When she sent him her photograph, she mentioned wearing Jim's gift then and on other special occasions (p. 77).
2    The heroic drama *Ben Hur* was adapted from the novel by General Lew Wallace's *Ben Hur; or, the Days of the Messiah* (1880). The book was described as 'a long and gorgeously colored romance of oriental life in the first century, abounding in florid scenes of pageantry. The plot is intricate and the grammar is not always faultless'. Ernest A. Baker, *A Guide to Historical Fiction* (London, 1914), p. 395. After the play opened on Broadway in 1899, it toured the country for twenty years. In its Boston production (20 December 1900), there was a cast of 350 and an on-stage race of twelve horses.

# *1902*

✶

[Pittsburgh, Pa.]
January 11, 1902

My dear Jim,

It is *almost* time that I should acknowledge your letter, but it is
not through forgetfulness that I did not do so. We have been kept
pretty busy since I wrote you last, and I have not dropped a line
to a creature since the holidays. Xmas time is so very busy with
us taking the children to parties and so forth, and I am glad its all
over now.

Our folks are getting ready for Florida. We expect to leave here
about the first week of February. I have no idea yet how far south
we are going, so you see we do not stay long in Pittsburgh for which
I am very glad, as I am not dead in love with it. Though all my
friends are here, it would not cost me a thought to go a thousand
miles away from it. I don't wear out my welcome.

When I was penniless and alone the day you left me at the Union
depot, soon after that I found who my future friends would be.
They were *very very few*, so do you blame me for being reserved
and independent now. You will consider me hard for writing such a
sentence I know, but I have to say what I think to one whom I
consider a friend. The old saying let the past bury its dead should
be my rule, but unfortunately I am of the type that feels the sting
long after the bite.

Well, we had rather a pleasant Xmas beginning that beautiful morn by going to early mass which is the principal event of the day with us notwithstanding the long walk to the church after two hours sleep. We never get to bed before two on Christmas night owing to the decorating of the Xmas tree that Santa is supposed to bring the little ones. We all got very nice gifts. Indeed, everybody remembered us most kindly.

I am so sorry to have disappointed the Brooklyn brothers. I wish when your sister would write she would tell them, and if ever an opportunity be within my reach again, I assure you I'll try my hardest to see them. I hope all your friends are well. How nice it would be for your sister if she would try to become a trained hospital nurse, something which *I* will try someday to be.

I have not heard any more from you trying to get on the fire department. Jim, there is nothing like trying to elevate yourself. I have come to that conclusion a long time ago. Almost every morning when taking my boy to school, I pass by the engine house and never do I pass that house without thinking of you in connection with it though why I cannot tell. I always picture you in one of their rigs.[1]

You said you were coming to Pittsburgh, but not till summer. That seems so undecided!! Still, it is something for me to be looking forward to. This is about the 20th time I have started this letter, writing about a sentence each time.

Well, Jim, don't keep the answer to this as long as I did yours, for I'll be anxiously waiting for a line from you. My heart would be good enough to write you every day, so you see you have my good will as my nonsensical letters don't count much. Don't forget to write as soon as possible.

I am, Jim X

As ever same old Annie[2]

1   Fire Engine No. 14, Truck D, the local fire station, was located on Neville Street next to the Dusquesne Gardens.

2   Annie enclosed, but did not mention, a clipping about the Rt Rev. R. Phelan, Bishop of Pittsburgh since 1889. Annie bracketed the sentence that described Bishop Phelan's birth near Ballyragget, Co. Kilkenny. Bishop Phelan (1828–1904) was not related to the Phelans but Jim knew him. Conversation with Eileen Phelan (Sr M. Gabriel), 2 Mar. 2003. Bishop Phelan was born in Sralee, near Ballyragget, Co. Kilkenny. He served as Bishop of Pittsburgh, 1889–1904. His successor, Archbishop J. F. Regis Canevin, described Bishop Phelan as 'a man of prudent zeal and extraordinary business ability' (Msgr Francis Glenn, *Shepherds of the Faith 1843–1993: A Brief History of the Bishops of the Catholic Diocese of Pittsburgh* (Pittsburgh, 1993), p. 115.

---

2 FEBRUARY 1902

Bayard Street
[Pittsburgh, Pa.]
Feb. 2nd, 1902

My dear Jim,

I am alone today and having a few moments at my disposal. I thought I would drop you a few lines being the only chance I may have for doing so before going South.

All arrangements are made for leaving here on Saturday night, the 8th. The trip will be long and a rather dreary one. It was so when we had only two little Mellons, and I suppose it will be more so now with the third. But still we have each other and in that way, things become much lighter than otherwise. We relieve the monotony by a cup of tea at intervals prepared on our own little lamp which we have to carry with us everywhere to prepare the baby's food. I am not much of a tea drinker, but in travelling, I assure you, it is always welcome.

Well, I have a joke that I think too good to keep, so you must come in for your part. At Xmas, the custom in this house is to have a Santa Claus for the little ones. A suit of Mrs. Mellon stuffed represents the good old fellow. Then a good natured-looking face of Santa's with a brown hood comprises the whole thing. Then he takes his place by his tree till the night on which he is supposed to take the whole business away.

Well, this was the night I had the joke on one, or in fact all the girls, in the house. Then the family heard the laughing and of course had to be told the cause. I took the old fellow (not very easily carried) downstairs and seated him in the dining room, then called on each of the girls in turn, and maybe there was't some tall laughing going on. That part went very well till the night following when secretly I went upstairs to the girls' room and put Santa's face in one of the beds. I told no one. In fact, it passed entirely off my mind till Ellen and I were having a little chat by the nursery fire just before going to bed, and of course on hearing those merry peals of laughter from above, guessed the cause.

It scared her at first, but then she saw the funny side of it and blamed me right away for doing it. For days after it had been the general topic. So one day she turned the joke on me, and in my absence came into my room and took your picture (which she must have thought was my greatest prize then on exhibition) and kept it till just a few days ago. Now it is in the same old place till someone else comes and tries to run off with it. Well, Jim, taking the serious side of it, we are all very happy. The girls are all very nice.

Perhaps, Jim, it would be just as well if you didn't try for the fire department. if you can see any other way for improving yourself. You have a nice education, and I don't think it would be very hard for you to push yourself through. Of course you know best, and you can see where your chances lie. There is nothing like having ambition and determination. Those are two qualities that I am sorry to say I lack in to a certain extent.

But now I have plucked up courage enough to say I will try to become a hospital nurse. One of the best doctors in Pittsburgh has a deep interest in me and thinks I will have no difficulty in getting through. Wouldn't you be glad if I were so fortunate?

About that little scene in Philadelphia, I don't think I will ever forget it, for I cannot tell why that gentleman's generosity was so bountiful that night, first giving me a quarter and then having a bag of *All Sorts* filled for me.[1] I have told that tale over and over, and people told me I was doing 'first rate in America', but, Jim, I have to tell you *it* was the only money I handled for many a day after coming here.[2]

Loyalty was something I always honoured and my first thought when I get rested here, was to write a few lines to *some dear friends* in Galway, and, of course, that was not quite right in my friends' eyes, but I am genuine to the core if I once say, 'I am your friend', then I am *one*, staunch and true to the last, come what may. So few people understand my nature. Ellen is the only one outside Ireland's few that understands me thoroughly, and she would do anything on earth for me. Is it then any wonder that I like her so?

Do you mind poor Jim from Mayo? I often wonder what has become of him and his mother, poor old lady. Do you remember the night we were on the train? She thought it was so good to be able to talk to her in her native language. If I had that time to live over again, I would have been much better to her as I know a good deal more now than I did then.

Well, it is pretty near time that I should bring my newspaper to a close. I had no intention of writing so much when I started. You will address your letters here till you hear from me again. I hope to hear from you before I leave, but if not it will be all the more welcome when we will be 'lone' 'all alone' in the crowded hotel.

So now
a fond
good bye
and remain
as ever Annie

1    The gentleman gave Annie a bag of assorted liquorice candies which were (and still are) known in Ireland and Britain as Allsorts. The sweets were made by an English firm called Bassett's.

2    According to the List or Manifest of Alien Immigrants for the *Adria* sailing from Queenstown 27 October 1898, Annie arrived in Philadelphia with $10.

---

*c*.20 FEBRUARY 1902

[Florida][1]

. . . in Nov. to see about the big boat now in construction and we may go soon after.[2] How nice if your pictures were at the Royal Palm to greet me, but I hope to have the pleasure of seeing the real one before that time.

Well now I must finish as I have to go on the beach with the children and often whilst on the sands my thoughts take a long journey and am often reminded of you by Ellen. You don't know how glad she would be to see you, for every time I get your letters, she says so many nice things about you and is always anxious to know when you are coming.

Now do write soon as I will be expecting one soon and perhaps in the next letter I will be able to state some of our plans. Always remember me kindly to your people and with best love for yourself,

Am as ever Annie[3]

Am in a hurry x.

1    Fragment of a note on 3 x 5 in. scrap of paper. Envelope: Hotel Indian River, Rockledge, Florida. In 1893 Henry Flagler took his railroad as far south as Rockledge. Henry Morrison Flagler (1830–1913) was the Standard Oil and railroad tycoon who developed south Florida and built the Royal Palm Hotel on 15 acres along Biscayne Bay in Miami in 1896. The hotel had 450 guest rooms.

2    The boat was the *Vagabondia*, the first of W. L. Mellon's series of increasingly lavish yachts by that name.

3    Annie enclosed two clippings: an article titled 'Outings for traction men' describing a two-day outing at Calhoun Park for the employees of the United Traction Company, and

'All sorts', a humorous poem about the outing with a drawing of a traction man with a girl on his arm. The traction men worked on the inclined plane railways that were built around Pittsburgh between 1870 and 1901. Electric streetcars in the 1890s challenged but did not replace the inclined plane railways.

---

14 MARCH 1902

Hotel Royal Palm
Miami, Florida
March 14th 1902

My dear Jim,

You see by the above address we are no longer at Rockledge. We left there about the 26th Feb. and are now stationed at the Royal Palm Hotel, Miami, a place about 350 miles further south. Rockledge was a beautiful place but sinks into nothing where Miami is concerned.

In the first place, it is not such a favourite place being on a cheaper scale whilst this place is actually the centre of gaiety and wealth. The big hotel with its beautiful gardens and tropical fruits and flowers all in one is an earthly paradise. We are only a short way from Cuba and the West Indies, so if we keep on, we will soon be at the equator. I tell you it feels like that now, for dressed in the lightest summer wear, we are almost baked. I often say to Ellen, 'Is roasting to death or freezing to death the worst?'

Anyhow, we are having a delightful time, lots more company to help pass away the time, lots of both indoor and outdoor amusements and music at different times during the day and always at night. It is a grand band employed by all the hotels of the Flagler system.[1]

We are situated directly on the Bay whilst the ocean is only a short distance across. This is the home of the coconut, dates, bamboo etc. We saw some Indians a few days ago.[2] They live out in the woods about ten miles from here. We have lots of driving, have a carriage most afternoons. Sometimes we visit very interesting places. One in particular was where the soldiers of the Spanish–American War camped.[3]

We have a dear little church here and a Jesuit Father, such a home-like little place. He is the first Jesuit I met since I left my good friend Rev. O'Donovan, S.J. in Galway.[4]

This is a little souvenir of my Florida trip, to show you that amongst all this gay, gorgeous place I don't forget, and I wish you would write me soon as I may not be long here, and it takes so long to reach us. I got your last letter all right being forwarded from Rockledge. Must now finish and please excuse this scribble. Address to the same old Annie

   c/o W. L. Mellon

   Hotel Royal Palm

   Miami, Florida


P.S. Hope you will have a good Patrick's Day. Write very soon –[5]

1   The Flagler hotels offered their guests an elaborate social life. The highlight of Miami society was Flagler's Washington's Birthday Ball. Edward N. Akin, *Flagler: Rockefeller Partner and Florida Baron* (Kent, OH, 1988), p. 163.

2   The Royal Palm was built on the site of a Seminole Indian mound.

3   Henry Flagler gave two lots on the corner of 8th Street and Avenue D for an encampment site for the soldiers of the Spanish-American war. John Sewell, *Miami Memoirs* (Miami, 1987), p. 132.

4   The Church of the Holy Name was completed in 1898 on land donated by Henry Flagler. It was replaced in 1925 by the Gesu Church. The Jesuit priest was Father Fountain, the priest who founded Holy Name. There are photographs of the church and Father Fountain in Sewell.

5   Annie enclosed the letterhead from the Hotel Royal Palm that had a drawing of the hotel. She added the note, 'A picture of the Hotel we are staying at.'

26 MARCH 1902

Hotel Royal Palm
Miami, Fla.
Wednesday night

Dear Jim,

A few lines just to let you know I have not entirely forgotten you as I fear you did not receive my parcel of the 14th which has worried me very much indeed as I had a note enclosed. I am sure I put your address on properly. I wish you would write by return if possible so that I may see to it before leaving which we expect to on Tuesday next.

I must hurry for the mail, and I am *so sorry* for leaving here. I don't know what to do. I had such a delightful time. Excuse this hurried note and don't notice the writing.

Hope to hear from you *very soon*.

remain as ever
Annie

Address:
A. O'Donnell
c/o W. L. Mellon
Hotel Royal Palm
Miami
Florida

———

27 MARCH 1902

Royal Hotel Palm
Thursday night

My dear Jim,

Your letter reached me this morning. Am sorry now I had not more patience and waited a little longer, but the fact of us leaving here so soon made me quite anxious as to whether the parcel was sent all right as the clerks here are not over anxious about things. Mrs. Mellon complained only a few days ago about a letter of hers that was forwarded to Boston. Of course, I know this is an immense place that requires constant attention to see things are in order. I am so glad you liked it all right. I wanted you to have some rememberance [*sic*] from Miami.

Well, I am sorry for leaving as I never enjoyed myself better. Always had a good time. The people I met were very nice. In most every walk of life there comes the time for that sad word good bye, but still such is life.

We go from here to a place called Palatka.[1] Moving north and coming nearer home, but before we get to Pittsburgh we expect to go to New York for a few weeks, and I guess we will not leave Florida before 15th April. The fact of us going to be some time in New York will, I hope, enable me to see your cousins in Brooklyn, as I will make an extra effort to get them this time.

What do you suppose a few days ago Mrs. Mellon gave me a nice new camera, and I must say am most busy taking pictures. I have a few at the office to be developed. Perhaps I will send you some if they are good. I was so glad. You too are having the *picture craze* – but poor me must always have some kind of craze, and it might as well be one as another.

I hope you will write me soon and excuse my hasty address this time.

Annie
c/o J. R. Mellon
Palatka
Florida
Good night as ever fondly.
Annie

1    One of the oldest settlements on the St John's River, Palatka (*pilakilkaha*, crossing over), was a popular resort after the Civil War. WPA, *The WPA Guide to Florida* (New York, 1984[1939]), p. 353. Nevin Winter described travelling on the St John's River above Palatka. 'The St John's River narrows and its beauty intensifies. The small steamer winds its way under the experienced eye of a thoroughly trained pilot, following the navigable channel that winds about through a vegetation of the most picturesque and wonderful sort conceivable.' Nevin Winter, *Florida: The Land of Enchantment* (Boston, 1918).

---

10 APRIL 1902

[Palatka, Florida]
April 10th, 1902

My dear Jim,

Your letter reached me on Wednesday, 2nd, just a few minutes before leaving the hotel. The picture has never turned up yet, and imagine the disappointment having to leave the Hotel before it arrived. Still, I lived in hopes that it would be sent here as Mr. Mellon left orders with the clerk to send all mail to our Palatka address. Whether the picture came there or not, I cannot tell. I put off writing to you till now hoping it would come in the meantime. And we are leaving here tomorrow. Just think how things will happen. The post office certainly is not in our favour. You don't know *how* disappointed I feel, for I did look forward with the greatest hopes of seeing it about a day or so after coming here at the very most.

We expect to spend a day or so at Jacksonville and then go to New York, where we can only stay about three days. We hope to be in Pittsburgh before the 18th, much sooner than was expected. I am glad we are leaving here for I assure you it is not much but the grandparents [who] have a cottage and will have the children spend a week or so with them when they can.[1] Of course, that is perfectly natural.

Palatka is nice enough for old people that look for quietness, for anything else, I cannot see where it comes. Of course it would never suit our folks, and I am mighty glad of it, but if I should live to be an old lady, never will I forget my time at the *paradise Miami*. I don't know when I was more happy or had a better time, and on our way to the station that Wednesday morning, how eagerly I looked at the many places where I had such a pleasant time, and wondered if I should ever see them again.

My pictures turned out pretty nice for a beginner. There are some I must send you, but can't get them now. Perhaps the next time I write, I will send them.

You had better write your answer to this to Pittsburgh and hope by that time your picture will come from some source, for it is only Ellen that knows how anxious I am about it.

I was much disappointed when I was told how short our New York visit is expected to be. I looked to seeing your friends in Brooklyn as Mrs. Mellon said first she would spend a week there. I will be glad to get back once more to Smoky City, but we will be there about a month when we will be off again to Spring Lake, perhaps the first week in June. So you must hurry up and try [to] come soon.

Ellen and I get a week or so each when we come home from the South each year. Mrs. Mellon is very kind in matters of that sort. She knows how we have done with the children night and day since we left Pittsburgh, so recompenses us by giving a vacation which I think is very good.

I have not anything so very interesting as usual, but nonsense which I must bring to a finish, hoping you will excuse *writing* etc. as this table seems to be suffering from palsy. So Jim, please write as soon as *you* know anything of the picture.

As ever fondly I remain, Annie

Just as I had finished this letter, yours was handed to me, and these pictures I found at the same time. Two of them I took myself and some busy body picked up the camera and took Ellen and I under the shading branches of a coconut palm when I least expected, so you see for yourself. I don't suppose you could tell from it which is which but to avoid mistake, the taller of the two is I. Again I will say good-bye and sincerely hope that yours will show up soon.

Am as ever

Annie

1    The J. R. Mellons and the Matthew Taylors wintered in Palatka. W. L. Mellon met Mary Hill (May) Taylor in Palatka; they were married there in March 1896.

---

23? APRIL 1902

Pittsburgh, Pa.
Wednesday night

My dear Jim,

We arrived here from New York on Friday morning last after one of the hardest nights I ever had on a train. I thought Ellen would never live to see Pittsburgh. She was feeling fine till the day we left New York when she complained on a pain in her side, but before we were very long on the train, dysentery was running its course coming to a pretty bad stage before morning. We had the doctor directly we come home. Mrs. Mellon then got a trained hospital nurse as Ellen seemed to be getting very weak and suffering actual agony.

I thought several times she was dying, but thank the good Lord she is a little better tonight. It is hard while I write this to hear her whom I dearly love moaning in the next room. It has taken all my strength to keep up, for what shall I do if she leaves me? You know it is most remarkable in my case, ever since I can remember, if I have a happy time something is liable, in fact, bound to *make* turn up that will shatter all that happiness away, but I look at things as sent by Heaven and they will in their own time turn out perhaps *for the best . . . !*

I have not seen any one my friends since I came home. Your picture was the only consolation I have had and sick as poor Ellen was, I showed it to her, but she said nothing. *Tears spoke instead.* She breaks down completely as soon as I enter her room.

Well, Jim, your picture is indeed fine. I am so pleased with it as it does a good deal more justice to you than the first. You have gotten very stout and look pretty near like 'that boy I addressed for the first time on the deck of the tender.' If I get the other two, I won't promise to send them back, but I *might* give them to you when you come here.

Now when this long promised visit is decided on, I am afraid there must be promises on both sides in regard to our correspondence, as your letters are presentable where mine are not. I don't care who sees yours, but please burn them, for I never think twice, and you get on paper exactly what I am. Still we will leave that aside for further consideration.

I am glad to see by your letter that *you* at least think me unchangeable. Looks have not altered for the better, but I am whom time can never change and so few people understand, and if Ellen should become worse, then I am alone.

I am sure the Brooklyn cousins will think I am not a lady of my word. I am ashamed to think I had to give up going each time I promised, but I cannot be blamed, for before I say a thing, [I] am pretty near sure of carrying it out, be it ever so small. I hope they will understand.

Well, dear Jim, [I] must now say good night and hope you will write me soon, for every letter is now appreciated to cheer me up and as ever

I fondly remain Annie

———————

### 3? MAY 1902

[Pittsburgh, Pa.]
Saturday night

My dear Jim,

Many thanks for your nice letter which I have not been able to answer till now, but be assured I appreciate it more than I can tell. I am very glad to say Ellen is very much better. Just think how delighted I was to have her with me in the nursery today (for the first time), but she is frightfully weak and will be for some time. I have her with me now, and if by sacrificing time and pleasure, I am willing to do both if that will but help her. I read her your letter and she did think it kind of you and your aunt to remember us. I rather envy you to have such a nice good woman to whom you can say what you feel like – so much like a Mother!

There is a girl here from very near my house, but as yet have not had a chance to see her. I am just crazy to have a talk with her about my dear home and parents. I believe my youngest brother will soon come here too. He is only a young lad about 18. Then the old homestead will be rid of us all excepting my oldest brother.[1] Is it not too bad to see such a sad scene? As soon as a boy or girl gets big enough to help the house, he is forced to leave perhaps never again to see those dear ones and would give anything in after years for one hour of that innocent happy fun known only in their dear old homes.

I don't believe all this talking we read about will ever help Ireland[.][2] Too much talk is not good in matters of that kind. 'Actions speak louder than words.' The Irish race are too deceitful to each other for any good. It takes more than speeches to affect J. Bull's tyranny. But 'every dog has his day.' Perhaps his is coming.

The kind of weather we are now having reminds me of Florida. I was just thinking how nice it would be to have you here now. Everything looks so nice. But I feel as if you will not be able to come. I am sorry to think that, for how long I have looked to this

month or June, and yet you seem as far off now as ever. I understand circumstances and must not be too rash, so *you* know best.
You do just what is most fit and God direct us all. He always does
the right.

I hope those pictures are not in the Royal Palm. They are sure to
be done away with. Too bad we did not stay there longer. Still I am
glad to have one. It really is a very good one of you, but I think you
were in a serious mood when they were taken. Even Ellen noticed
that. I think you are unnatural when looking serious. You were
always the life of that crowd on the *Adria*. I wonder what has
become of them all?

I think this little enclosed piece is worth looking over when you
have time.[3] I wish one of them would extend his politeness and let
you off for a week.

Well I *do* suppose it is time to give up just now as I think you will
be tired reading when you get through my little newspaper. Now
write very soon and tell me all the news and remember me very
kindly to your aunt and sister. Hoping to hear from you *very* soon.
I now say a fond good night.

1    Annie's older brother Pat stayed on in the Lippa homestead. Born on 9 March 1864, he
died in 1932 and is buried in the cemetery in Cnoc.
2    It is not clear what Annie means when she refers to talk about helping Ireland. It may
have something to do with the United Irish League which was founded in New York in
December 1902 or with the resolution of problems within Irish-American organisations
like the Ancient Order of Hibernians.
3    Enclosure: undated newspaper cutting, 'Rah! Rah! Rah! Trolley Cars' which describes
college boys working on the trolleys to Coney Island during summer vacation.

[Pittsburgh, Pa.]
Thursday

My dear Jim,

Is it not too bad that you could not get here for even a few days! I think those streetcar managers are the meanest fellows on earth not to allow you off. I am no doubt disappointed as I so long and earnestly hoped of seeing you. Ellen and I were busy thinking all week what we could do for you when you came. But I guess it cannot be helped. I know you would not disappoint me without sufficient reason. At least I think not.

I have looked at it in this light – that you did not see a suitable time just now for a holiday or you would come, but remember, you will be always welcome, and as you say, 'Perhaps, it is all for the best.' Heaven alone knows. Those late years I look at things as sent by Providence with a good intent, and until I change my opinion of you (which *I hope will never be*), I still will hope that we will meet, be it ever so long to wait for.

We don't expect to leave for Spring Lake before July 1st as Mr. Mellon is quite busy with the new mansion he is having built which when completed will be one of the finest residences in Pittsburgh.[1] I don't suppose we will be back before October, that is if we take our usual trip to the mountains.

The weather is certainly trying to push on to the lake as it is about hot enough now for anyone. When it becomes so *very* hot, Mrs. Mellon gets the porch fixed for us so that we could eat there and in the evenings when work is done, we all get together and have lots of fun. There are five of us girls and two coachmen. We only kept one man in the stable till lately. Now that there are more horses and an auto, there is plenty of work to keep two going. We drive almost every afternoon to the parks with the children.

That was a grand turn out you had in Indianapolis. It was very interesting to read about it. I am so glad you sent that paper as both Ellen and I are deeply interested in such things.

We are very busy now preparing for the summer. Mrs. Mellon supplies everything and we do the sewing. We have everything white for the morning and black in afternoon. I think I was a fortunate girl the day I got into this family for it's one of the best houses in the city. They are kind and will never let a small thing done for them go unrewarded, so that it is a pleasure to work for them.

I have often wondered how your sister is doing, though I never mentioned it. You will have a nice time now that you can go cycling. It is so nice you are together.

Well, I think I now must bring to a finish as there is nothing of interest to relate, so hoping you won't forget me entirely and I *ask you to write soon.*

Will now remain, fondly as ever Annie

P.S. Remember me to all. Yes, give but one passing thought to me, Jim.

---

1  W. L. Mellon's 45-room mansion Ben Elm was built on five and a half acres at the corner of Darlington Avenue and Forbes Street in the Squirrel Hill section of the city. Ben Elm was demolished in 1951. Only the pillars of the gate remain. (David E. Koskoff, *The Mellons: The Chronicle of America's Richest Family* (New York, 1978), p. 461.

---

5 JUNE 1902

New York
June 5th 1902

Address next letter
c/o W.L. Mellon
Spring Lake
New Jersey

My dear Jim,

You didn't expect an answer from this part of the world I am sure. Did you ever notice anything half so mean as the way things have turned out since we counted on meeting each other? Now that you are ready to come here, I am stuck in New York with the three children. I just wonder what have I ever done that such disappointments should lay in wait for me.

Our reason for running away from home was due to an epidemic of measles and scarlet fever which are at present raging in our neighbourhood, so on Monday night last Mr. Mellon thought it wise to send the little ones on here with Mrs. Mellon and I and leave Ellen with the girls to look after the entire packing and then go straight to the Spring Lake cottage where we will all meet on Saturday.

I am so mad to think I was so near seeing you and *now so far*. How things will happen. I suppose we were not destined to meet yet. Let us blame it on destiny anyhow and claim it's all for the best. What a poor consolation. And when do you suppose we will meet now, just when the good Lord wishes. I think is the best answer. I cannot get over the way we had to rush not even time to say goodbye to a few friends. Some of them don't know, but what I am still in Pittsburgh, and, if you please, I had my picture taken on Thursday preceding Decoration Day and had to come away without seeing what they look like. No proof came yet.

I think I am pretty brave to bear all that, and yet the hardest of all came with your letter this morning. I just hate to think you will come now when I am so far away. I can just imagine myself if I were in Pittsburgh this morning and got your letter. My, how I would hustle around and how eagerly I would wait for that day to see you, but in a word I guess *such is life* at least for some.

I will be so glad to get your sister's picture. Don't forget to send me one as soon as you can. There is a friend of mine in Pittsburgh who spent some five years in Indianapolis as a contractor. He gave me quite an account of the city which was very interesting indeed. From all accounts, it is not as dirty as Pittsburgh.

Well, Jim, I am so tired now and it is so late and with two youngsters to sleep with, I better retire. You know I have a little picnic of my own trying to manage the three, but Mrs. Mellon is very good. She helps a good bit. Maybe I don't miss Ellen. I miss her more and more each time.

I hope this will reach you before you make any arrangements for your supposed trip. I get any amount of teasing about your letters. Even the mailman wants to know how *Indiana* is! But I am quite a good hand at teasing myself, so I must not mind it.

The heat is somewhat terrific here. When I was out this afternoon and saw those poor motormen standing in the cars, my thoughts went straight to you and couldn't help but feel for you out in all weathers.

Write me very soon. Writing now is the only consolation left, so try and let me know how you are doing. Remember a note from you is highly prized, and you cannot send them too often. I have a kindly feeling for you, and come what may it can never be severed. This alone is all I can boast of, and I must say it is this real sincere friendship that has gained me such good friends. I am glad to think I can count on you as one. So now, dear Jim, with best love I say a fond good-night and do write soon. x

―――――――

12 JUNE 1902

Windmere
Spring Lake, N.J.
June 12, 1902

My dear Jim,

As I was sitting this morning on the beach my thought strayed back to some days gone by and I cannot but have a kindly feeling for Spring Lake, (bleak and lonely as it now appears), for it was here that your first letter found me.

We got here all right on Saturday last. Have had perfect weather since, ocean perfectly beautiful but the boardwalk and beach very deserted looking and only a few cottages occupied. The season has not yet commenced. None of the big hotels are yet open and till then, which will be towards the end of this month, this will be quite lovely.

Well, on returning from our morning outing, I found your letter waiting for me. Glad I was when I saw it, but when I read it, my thoughts took a different turn, for I so anxiously looked for a cheering letter from you, as there is nothing it seems will cheer me those days.

Ellen has told me time and time again to look at the sunny side of things, but even *she* has failed, so I read her part of your letter today, and her consoling words were, 'true love never *did* run smooth'. But I might feel a little happier by cheering up and asking you to still have hope. We are not so terribly far apart when you come to think of it, so in the fall if you could then get off for some time, we will make up for all.

You see, I didn't get a vacation which was due me owing to Ellen's sickness, but come what may I will get one when we get home which will be probably in September owing to our getting away so early. I guess by then we will be tanned enough. I am three shades browner since I came here and the children are almost black.

Ellen wishes me to impress it on you not to take any days off till then. She is very anxious to see you and would be more than delighted to see my one wish gratified, and if she had anything to do with it, she would have paved a way long ago for us to see each other once again. She would do anything to see me happy even at her own expense. I only wish you could spend some time with us on this delightful beach. Then indeed would our happiness be complete. It is too bad to think such cannot be.

Well, Jim, one sentence in your letter made up for a good deal, '*proof of my fidelity.*' I am glad to know you think that I am true, for when I cannot say that which I often would wish to, you can still judge for yourself that in my case 'actions would speak louder than words'. Even with Ellen, whom I dearly love, my words on the subject are but few. Still she knows that she is one of those very few dear ones, and though I have changed in looks quite a good deal since you saw me, I think I still am that same old Annie.

I got the proofs of my picture. They are not so bad but could be a little better. They may be finished soon, and of course you shall have one.

Since I started writing this note, Mrs. Mellon called me to say she had raised all our wages, a little recompense for the inconvenience that we had to suffer from coming away so quickly from home.

Now it is quite late as usual and must hurry, and I ask you especially to write me soon. Just even a few lines will satisfy if you will but write soon and help me forget the gloomy past which will come too often before me in this beautiful but sad spot alone by the wave-washed shore. And don't forget me who was the very *best* of that little group on the *Adria* so that will say a fond

Good Night

And *will* remain, with love

Annie

----

24 JUNE 1902

Spring Lake [New Jersey]
Tuesday night

My dear Jim,

I surely thought my picture would be here by this time, but as yet none have shown up, and even when they do come, I doubt that they will be particularly good. I shall send them out though that you might be able to distinguish me if that be possible, when we meet – if nothing else occurs to shatter those hopes we now realize. Won't it be terrible if we meet like strangers, for I assure you I am not much like the girl you saw on that blessed *Adria* as you will see when you get my picture.

I often picture myself waiting for you at the station, but I always pride myself on the fact that I *will* know you. Don't you wish the months would hurry up and why does time drag *so* slowly when you are anticipating any event? Ellen and I often have little talks about such incidents. She certainly likes you as she delights in hearing about you.

Spring Lake is becoming quite gay now. The hotels and casinos being opened since Saturday and quite a number of the cottages occupied, and from the merry peals of laughter on the boardwalk, it sounds like old times. This is the customary place for the boys and girls to meet after work is done.

A beautiful new church has taken the place of our old one.[1] It was donated by a Mr. Maloney in memory of his little daughter who died here some few years ago. No money was spared to make it the admiration of all, and people of every denomination speak of it as a credit to the worthy gentleman. It is most gorgeous throughout, everything being of the richest kind. I am just in love with it reminding me so much of the Dominican Church in Galway.[2] We go to mass every Sunday, the only consolation we have here, and I remember you in my poor prayers now. Even though I am far away, you see I still remember, and if you knew how I appreciated your effort in answering my last letter *soon* as I had asked you. I think you were pretty nice. You know I look forward to a few lines from you as I know you have not much time at your disposal.

What delightful nights these are for bicycle riding. We must soon treat ourselves to a few. I don't care for going alone, and Ellen, as yet, does not like to risk it, but I think soon she will be well enough to ride.

I have been thinking so much lately of the hospital and cannot come to a conclusion what to do. I dread the period of three years more than the work for my heart goes straight out to anyone in pain. I consider nursing the noblest work one can do, but I fear three years steady work would outdo me completely especially when compared to my present occupation. Of course, if I don't try it by this fall, it's doubtful I ever will. If I could see any way for getting through in less than three years, I wouldn't hesitate a moment, but heaven direct me to the best is all I can say. I know that at present I am doing well. I could not have a better place, for we have everything as we make it ourselves. Nobody interferes and the highest wages are paid. Still, I suppose if that be my vocation, I will get there at all cost.

Well, dear Jim, I hope you are having good times there, and I suppose the weather must be warm, as it is nice here as yet. The nights are quite cool though, but beautiful on the beach. That lovely ocean. What a picture does it present these glorious moonlight nights. Now I must bring this letter to a finish and hoping to hear from you very soon. I will remain as ever Annie, and say a fond good-night and ask you to write soon to cheer this lonely heart, so good-night. x

1    Annie is referring to St Catherine's Church which was erected by the Papal Marquis Martin Maloney in memory of his younger daughter Catherine. The cornerstone was laid in 1901; the church was consecrated on 25 May 1902.

2    The Dominican church in Galway was St Mary's in the Claddagh. Annie would have
known the present church which was opened in 1891. (Eustás Ó Héideáin, *The Dominicans
in Galway* (Galway, 1991), p. 36).

---

11 JULY 1902

Spring Lake, N.J.
July 11, 1902

My dear Jim,

I am glad you were not waiting for my picture before you wrote as I
have only received them this afternoon. I am sending one and can
only say that it certainly looks like me. I would like you to tell me
candidly what you think of it.

I read that account of the accident and certainly thought it sad.
You must have felt it keenly. Those cars, however, always fill me
with horror when they go very fast. Two or three times already they
have given me a scare. Ellen told me to impress you strongly 'with
saying your prayers night and morning' and I myself believe in that
above all things, for just imagine the number of lives you have at
your hands depending on you, and a single slip would dash them
into 'kingdom come' before they could be aware of the fact. Still,
every walk of life has its own peculiar dangers, and not one is
exempt from it more than the other.

I have thought quite a good bit of you thinking to take up
canvassing. Don't be cross with me if I tell you not to, for if you
never had your feelings hurt, you certainly would stand a risk of it
then. If anyone gets a cool send off, it is poor agents, but if you
think it all right and be happy, why by all means do it as you know
more about the business than I do. You know if nobody else in
Pittsburgh cares to receive you, *I gladly will*, but it would hurt me
to think you would go round from house to house with not one kind
word to cheer you along. Still we must not consider our feelings too

much when we try to make a living in this weary world, and every cloud has its own silver lining and perhaps ours will shine yet.

Times here are pretty much the same, but the Fourth made a little more difference in this quiet spot. We had auto races, bicycle races and lots of fireworks in the daytime and at night quite a display of electric fireworks. The soldiers are coming tomorrow to Sea Girt. They will enliven the place a bit.[1]

I busy myself these nights with copying *poetry*. Such pieces as strike me I keep in my little book. Enclosed is one or two, probably you have seen one with me on the *Adria* as I always kept it by me. It was composed by a schoolmate of mine and entitled 'When far away'![2]

As usual I am quite late and must now bring to a finish, hoping to hear from you very soon, so a fond good-night. I remain as ever,

Annie

x

1  4 July 1902 celebration in Spring Lake. The army encampment was in Sea Girt.
2  The poem is lost.

---

7? AUGUST 1902

Spring Lake, N.J.
Thursday night

Dear Jim,

I am very sorry to see by your letter that your sister has gone so far away from you notwithstanding your efforts to be together. It must have come hard on both, but you see that the nearest and dearest *must* part, and I feel sorry for her, poor girl, if she has to go among strangers, for in this weary world, there is not much to depend on.

You know when I first started out in Pittsburgh there was no one willing to give me a helping hand. On the contrary, [they] tried to push me down in my superior's estimation because I had just landed!! Still, I pulled through all after my poor heart was nearly broken, and those who were meanest to me then, now envy me my position. I wish your sister had come to Pittsburgh instead of going in the opposite direction.[1] I at least would do my best to help her and then perhaps you would come and see us. Our city is not very prepossessing but it is the best yet for work and wages.

Has your sister gone to Iowa for good or only for the summer? I hope you will write to her often, for a nice letter when one is lonely helps a good deal and always remember me to her.

We had quite a day at Sea Girt on 24th. The President visited the Camp as was anticipated, and everything was done so well that the boys in blue really did deserve credit for once. We all went out and had a good look at Roosevelt, and we did have a glorious time.[2]

The soldiers will soon be going home now, so that there is very little left in Spring Lake to make it lively. For some reason this has been the worst summer for both hotels and cottages. About one half are vacant and at times it looks quite deserted, more like late fall than its busiest season. Ellen and I had an afternoon off last week. We went to Asbury Park thence to Pleasure Bay by trolley. We had a delightful time and enjoyed our ride immensely.[3]

Well, Jim, I did fail to catch the meaning of that sentence in your last letter although why I cannot tell as you wrote it plain enough. It would be a joke, but I rarely answer the door bell. Still, I wish you would spring a surprise on us one of these days. Of course, I am glad you liked my picture, and hope you noticed your gift which I only wear on special occasions.

Now don't you worry too hard about your sister. Remember there is no *real* happiness in this world, for are we not every year – nay – every day – parting from some loved one. Still, God brings everything about in his own good way, and I think trust in Him is always the best, so you cheer up now, and let us hope that there is at least *one ray* of happiness in store for us. Every cloud has its silver lining and perhaps ours will yet shine.

I hope you will excuse grammar and all mistakes as the girls guessed who I was writing to, so they suggested all kinds of things to tell you.

Do write me soon and do you know that on 3rd August one year ago, your first letter reached me written on 20th July.[4] I saw it last night when looking through my diary. Now must finish for this time hoping to hear from you real soon.

I say a fond good night and remain as ever Annie
with love.                                                                          x.

1    Lena Phelan moved to Iowa where she married.
2    Theodore Roosevelt visited the soldiers' encampment during his cruise on the *Mayflower*, his official vessel that was converted from a dispatch boat. Fog delayed his return and he was marooned off Sea Girt. Edmund Morris, *Theodore Rex* (New York, 2001), pp. 127, 130.
3    During Annie's years at Spring Lake, Asbury Park would have been one of the most popular resorts on the New Jersey shore. Annie and Ellen would have been attracted by the city's boardwalk.
4    Annie's first letter was dated 2 August 1901 (p. 35).

---

1 SEPTEMBER 1902

Spring Lake
New Jersey
Sept. 1st

My dear Jim,

Enclosed you will find two pieces that will interest you when you have spare time to read them. Are you not sorry you are not a Pittsburgher? See how nice we are to the streecar men? I am sorry not to have been there to see the fun, but as far as I can see, we have no idea of leaving here. A week ago, they were planning to leave on the 17th. It is yet undecided whether we go to the country or not.

From the looks of Spring Lake at present, it is very evident that its season is nearing a close. I think this has been the coolest summer on record, and I guess the poor in large cities were glad of it. All of us girls had a day off to New York and we certainly enjoyed it. It was Mrs. Mellon's treat before going on a visit to Canada. She came back a few days ago and presented each with a pretty pin souvenir of the Coronation.[1]

I am glad your sister likes her new place, and I hope she will prosper. If she makes a *few* friends, it will be sufficient. I hope you won't take a notion and go there too. It sounds so far away.

Well, Jim, I am awfully glad you didn't happen to be one of those unfortunate fellows who were discharged. Don't ever learn to play those (*craps*). Just imagine a poor fellow working hard all week long and then turn over his money to those horrid dens. It is too bad, but as long as they exist, they will get lots of customers.

I have taken only a few pictures. It costs so much to have them developed, but I may be able to take some before leaving. We took the children to the ocean this morning. Maybe we didn't have a great time. This surf was beautiful, and now that the equinoctials have an effect on the Ocean making it appear like mountains. It presents one of the most beautiful pictures. This lasts for about ten days sometimes accompanied with very heavy rains and ocean storms.

I think the Royal Palm opens about November and Mr. and Mrs. are going to Florida [. . .][2]

1   Edward VII ascended the throne on 22 January 1901. His coronation was held on 26 June 1902.
2   The rest of the letter is missing.

---

Spring Lake [New Jersey]
Wednesday night

My dear Jim,

We will leave here on Tuesday next (16th), and it is a fixed date at last, but with that there are no bright prospects of a nice 'welcome home' as we are to go into a strange house, not our own dear little one where we had many a happy hour, but a large gloomy one away from Bayard Street. Mr. Mellon thought the family too large to be cramped in a small house like the one we all loved so well so that this new one will suit him till his own mansion be complete.[1] Ellen and I felt all upset today about the whole thing, for our cook will be with us no longer than while we are here. Still, we must try and adapt ourselves to circumstances, for we are happy as long as we remain together no matter who comes or goes.

We go from here to Philadelphia where we remain all day. Then we go on to the country where we expect to spend a week only and hope to be in Pittsburgh about the 27th September. My, but that sounds good! Just imagine what a long summer since 2nd June. Still, we didn't seem to notice the length so much as it was such pleasant weather.

I *do* hope your letter will reach here before I leave. Anyhow answer your next to Bayard Street as before, for our mail will be attended to after we get fixed in our new house, and be getting ready to pack your trunk, Jim. That's the only event I am looking forward to, your visit to the Smoky City.

While it is so awfully late, I must say good-night for the last time in Spring Lake this season. Hoping to hear from you soon. [I] remain with love,

Annie

1    The Mellons did not go to the rented house. They moved instead in April 1901 to the
Schenley Hotel till Ben Elm was ready (p. 98). Opened in 1898, the Schenley was called 'the
Waldorf of Pittsburgh'. The building is now the University of Pittsburgh's William Pitt
Union.

———————

19? SEPTEMBER 1902

[New Florence, Pa.]
Friday night

My dear Jim,

I will try to scribble a few lines by the light of a dull lamp, a *sure* sign
we are in the country. Nevertheless, it is none the less attractive. We
may not have all city conveniences, but we have nature's beauties to
see and admire. This mansion, built something after a castle style
and is a very antique design throughout, stands on a mountain
overlooking miles of beautiful country and surrounded by woods.[1]
The air is so pure and nice. In fact, I am in love with the place.

We are amusing ourselves at night with cards playing 'Old
Maid'. We are here alone with the children. Mr. and Mrs. Mellon
went straight to Pittsburgh, so we expect to be home about the 25th
if not before. Then I will get that long promised vacation whenever
you get ready to come, and *I will not let you* push the baby for I am
going to steer clear of them while you are in town.[2] You can see
them all, but I will be too glad to get away from them. We are both
looking for a little rest when things get straightened up a little, so
just write me a long letter *soon* and let me know when you can come
as you know Ellen and I will be looking forward to arranging our
time. She will be so glad to see you.

After all we are not leaving our nice old house at Bayard Street.
The one we were to have gone into was sold or had an offer of sale
in the meantime, and I am so glad.

Well, now, I *must* put up for the light is getting very dull, so
excuse all blots etc. and write as soon as you can. Give my kind

regards to your aunt and sister and hurry up before Jack Frost makes
his appearance, for it feels pretty much like him tonight. Pittsburgh
looks cold at all times but much more so when covered with snow
and smoke. I know you will be disappointed for I was very much so
till I got accustomed to it. Pittsburgh is like the people there. They
grow on you. It also has to grow, but you will soon see all.

So now good night and am expecting answer real soon.

As ever, Annie

1    Rachelwood, J. R. Mellon's mountain mansion near Ligonier, Pennsylvania, was
designed like a Bavarian castle. The 3,500-acre estate also included a church in the
wilderness. Koskoff, *The Mellons*, pp. 146–8. The buildings have been demolished; the land
is part of the Rachelwood Wildlife Research Preserve.
2    Jim may not have pushed the carriage, but he and Annie took the children to the zoo
(p. 91).

---

12 OCTOBER 1902

[Bayard Avenue,
Pittsburg, Pa.]
Sunday night
Oct. 12th 1902

My dear Jim,

A long, lonely week has come and gone since that dreary morn at
the Station.[1] I stood where you last saw me for a few minutes after
your train had gone, for I hated to face the city which had nothing
for me. Then, at last bracing up, I hurried to the car too much
occupied with my own thoughts to consider anything utterly
regardless of the rain which came down in torrents. Got home,
went up to my room, brave as if nothing had happened, donned my
uniform and took up my duties with 'smiles that could easily have
been tears'. What a long day it seemed to be, and how I longed for
night that I might rest, but when it came I laid my head down only
to realize more fully that good-bye is a very hard thing to say.

Sunday came but the memories of that previous morning were too much to be forgotten, and my head, how it did ache! Still I bore it all and said nothing but tried my hardest to appear my old self. The girls never ceased talking about you, Jim. They like you and expressed a great desire of seeing you again and wish to be always remembered to you. Talk about wishing *you* joy. They had me teased here, each one wondering what would be nicest in the line of gifts for me and were very anxious to know when is Jim going to send for you? It was indeed laughable. Mary teased me more than anyone. She was afraid I had gone with you. My only answer was, 'He is coming back!'

Your letter, Jim, was like talking to you again, and poor fellow, you did have a mean time getting in so late. I hope your cold is better. I know that morning you left here didn't help it any, and such has been the weather since then. The sun really condescended to shine a little while today. Is it *still raining*? I often wonder if it will ever clear up.

Mary left us on Thursday and we all felt so bad.[2] We had been such a happy little crowd those 3 years past, and she was so good to me. I appreciated kindness all the more because when I came here the cool way I was treated when I came to Pittsburgh was still fresh in my mind. My sisters and their people were under the impression that I came out here from school to depend solely on them. Penniless I was and independent I wanted to be, and far from being strong, as you know, my ambition was to find work as soon as possible before I should depend on cold charity. Long before I was able, I inquired of everyone about work till Heaven sent me to that big stone house I showed you. I surprised them all, for I was not so much of a city lassie with foolish notions after all.

I often wonder if I can ever forget, and now they all run with presents to me at different times, but when I needed help not one said, 'Here is a dollar, Annie.' Oh, why should I dwell on such a painful subject. I know I had and still have someone's good prayers. God has always been good to me in all things and I shall pray to Him, Jim, for you.

I miss you so much. Am alone and lonely tonight. Our new cook is sitting here with me. The other girls are out enjoying themselves. She is a County Mayo woman and appears to be so nice.

When have you heard from Lena? I guess by this time you have given all your friends a good description of the Smoky City. I hope you have remembered me kindly to your aunt and cousins. Try to persuade Lena to come here if she makes a change from where she is, for I think she would get along all right. I know when I did, most anyone can.

Well, I have not had the pleasure of a streetcar ride since then, but that 'Ding-ding' doesn't pass my notice though. I guess you are working as hard as ever now, but don't forget poor me. Consult that *wegie* [Ouija] board. This not spelled right, but you know, at your leisure, and if it says we will not meet again, *just break it*, for I had a very funny dream last night. Though not superstitious, I don't like it, but Heaven is our guide and in it are centered all my hopes.

Well, Jim dear, I must be finishing up hoping to have a letter from you as soon as you possibly can as a letter from you means so much to poor lonely me. So good night and believe me to always remain your own fondest Annie

God bless you  –  XXXXXXXXXXXXXXXXXXXXXXXXXXXXXXXXXXXXXXX

1    Jim visited sometime between 28 September and 5 October.

2    Mary O'Neill, the daughter of English parents born in Ireland, emigrated to the United States in 1880. A widow who had been married for four years, she is listed in the 1901 census as a chambermaid. *Twelfth Census of the United States*. Microfilm 351. M454.

3 NOVEMBER 1902

[4616 Bayard Street
Pittsburgh, Pa.]
Nov. 3rd 1902

My dear Jim,

When passing by your house today, I paused for a moment and thought a whole lot. Would to goodness that you were here again, but your letter is rather bright, and it may not be *very* long till we have a few days pleasure again, when I shall wait for you just where we parted. Hope it may be a more pleasant day or night.

Well, I was off yesterday and such a glorious day. Took advantage of such a rare occurrence and went to see friends. Talk about that ride to Westinghouse![1] It wasn't in it with yesterday's. I was pretty nearly squashed against the door. I held the strap and one of the sudden jerks caused a woman of 200 or 300 pounds to come spinning against me. I had to do the laughing myself, and maybe I didn't think of our rides together. Anyhow, I had a delightful time and enjoyed it very much.

I saw my sisters in the evening. They are well and asked for you very kindly, though they seem to think our acquaintance rather romantic to suit them, but, Jim, they can all think as they like. No words will change me and as you left me, so will I remain till you come back only be *true* to me and the confidence I have had in you since we first met is redoubled now. Heaven will guide us.

Write to me often. Nothing gives me greater pleasure. Indeed, I did turn away many a time disappointed whilst waiting for your letter till one morning (a week today). Just as I was going to school, I got it. Hope you have heard from Helena since then.

We had a gay time on Halloween. I dressed up and scared the girls. Unknown to all, I went out the cellar door and came in as they were eating supper.

We have another cook now. The last one didn't suit. This one is a Swede, a very nice person. Mary came to see us twice. She is working quite near us here. She talked quite a good bit about you and all the girls wish to be kindly remembered to you.

Well, Jim, do write soon as you can and excuse my horrid pen. So now good night and believe me ever to remain your Annie. xxxx – And write me a long letter just as soon as you have time. Will be looking for it soon – [2]

1    If Annie and Jim went out to Westinghouse Avenue, it would have been a long ride east towards Mckeesport.
2    Annie enclosed a scrap of newspaper, a ¾ in. x 2 ¼ in. drawing of a woman weeping as a man disappears over the horizon. Annie wrote on the corner, 'What does this remind you of?'

---

17 NOVEMBER 1902

[4616 Bayard Avenue
Pittsburgh, Pa.]
Nov. 17, 1902

My dear Jim,

I cannot tell you how glad I was to know that you consulted the doctor about your cough. Though it may have appeared too trifling in the start to bother about, still a little attention at first is worth a good deal afterwards, but you will be all right. Sometimes it only requires a little attention to set matters right. Only don't you be so hard on yourself. Take things easier and remember your health is more important than anything else. Now, Jim, when you get this, I want you to let me know exactly how you are progressing as I will feel quite anxious till I hear from you again. I wish I could do something for you, if I could cheer you up a bit, but I feel too *sad* or *lonely* or something tonight to write even a cheery note.

It may be the dull, dark weather. At least I'll blame that, but we have had perfect weather for ever so long until today when we had the lights burning all this afternoon. It reminds me of the day after you arrived here, only you are missing. Jim, that was the happy week! I wonder when there will be one like it. Come again. It would be something to look forward to, but in your nice letter, I see that it will be *just when you can*, and you could not do me a greater favour than that of trusting me to remain faithful to you. No matter what's said, you will be *the one* I shall rely on. Nothing will ever win me but *kindness* and that's what softened my heart first towards you.

Mrs. Mellon treated us to tickets for the theatre last week, and maybe I didn't enjoy it. Such a jolly piece, 'Williams and Walker in Dahomey'.[1] Well, Jim, you could have heard me laugh for squares. In fact, the whole audience was but one continuous roar. Then on Friday night last, Ellen and I went to see Andrew Mack as Tom Moore. It was very good. [It was] my first time to hear Mack's captivating voice. I was enthusiastic over the whole piece, the scene being laid in Ireland. Now, you would have liked it as I know you like Moore. Poor fellow, his love affairs certainly did not run smooth, but nevertheless, his faithful lady gave up wealth etc. for him, a poor poet.[2] I think I would have done the same.

How are all your friends and have they talked much about me lately? Anyhow give them my regards always. Ellen and Rose wish to be most kindly remembered to you. Poor Ellen has had quite a time with her eyes and been to the doctor all week. We sew late every evening and that may have caused it. Now she is getting better.

Well, Jim dear, hoping you will be all right soon. I now must finish. Will be looking for an answer real soon. You see we all have our troubles in this world. It is always something. I often wonder why things *are* so, but Heaven knows best and fits each one to their own cross. Heaven has always been my friend and it is to the One above that I raise my heart and hands at night for you, poor though my prayers may be. So now, dear Jim, it is time I should say I will bid you a fond good night and will always remain your fondest Annie – xxxxxx

Write just as soon as you can –

1    George Walker (1873–1911) and Egbert Austin Williams (1874–1922) were a vaudeville team who used African tradition in their *In Dahomey*.
2    Nea (Hester Louise Tucker) met Tom Moore in St George's, Bermuda in 1804. She gave up her fortune for the poet.

———

9 DECEMBER 1902

[4616 Bayard Ave.
Pittsburgh, Pa.]
Tuesday night

My dear Jim,

This is the first night since I got your last letter that I felt able to answer it. I headed the sick list this time. Though not laid up in bed, I suffered the most intense pain from a swelled face resulting from a cold caught very probably one Sunday night coming home when it was trying to snow and rain at the same time.

It settled principally on my ear (the outside) which had to be lanced. My, what did I suffer! Poor Ellen was nurse and a good one too. I went around with my various duties as best I could, but am glad to say that I feel so much better tonight.

I thought of you a lot, Jim, and I hope *you* are well, so I must now finish hoping my next note may be longer, but you know you have my love anyhow and accept this scribble. Good night and write me soon.

fondly as ever Annie[1]

1    Annie enclosed a clipping entitled 'Golden Streets in Indianapolis' which described men washing gold out of gravel after gold was discovered in the gravel and sand thrown from a sewer excavation.

———————

22? DECEMBER 1902

[4616 Bayard Avenue
Pittsburgh, Pa.]
undated

My dear Jim,

Accept this little gift from me with all the best wishes Xmas can offer. If they are not the right size, Jim, you know I will have them exchanged any time.

We were living in hopes of having snow for Xmas, but the weather is quite warm today. I think snow adds so much more delight to the young folks especially where 'Santa Claus' is concerned.

We are having a busy time now arranging matters for the little children who look forward to that day as the principal one of the year, and often I look back when it was mine too, but now it seems that it has the opposite effect and makes me feel sad.

Well, dear Jim, all the girls join me in wishing you a 'Merry Xmas' and a bright prosperous New Year. And I send my best wishes to you and your friends.

I now remain
fondly Annie xxx

# *1903*

✳

[4616 Bayard St. E.E]
Pittsburgh, Pa.]
Tuesday Night

My dear Jim,

Since I got your letter yesterday morning, I have been looking for your Uncle every time the bell rang, but as yet he has not called. Still I will not give up hopes till I hear from you again. I will be somewhat disappointed if he doesn't come.

Well how am I to thank you for the very acceptable gift you sent me.[1] How nice of you to have it done, Jim. I like it, Jim, and so does everyone that saw it. I invited my friends here. They all thought it fine. Ellen is quite taken with the frame and wished that your face was somewhat 'round the corner in it. For the present I must pack it as our things will be moved from here while we are South and *I do not* want anything to happen to it in strangers' hands, for I value it too much.

Well, Jim, I am glad you had a nice Xmas, as I had the happiest one since I left home. Really, I cannot begin to tell you how pleasant every one made it for me. As to gifts, I never was wealthier in my life. Such a display as greeted me when we came home from early mass. Mrs. Mellon and the children were so very good this year to every one of us, and poor Mary that left us didn't forget to send a nice gift and among ourselves such a jolly time as we did have.

It was the first Xmas that I can say I was really and truly happy in America.

Preparations for Florida are fast being made. Just think we expect to leave here about the end of this month, so we are not coming back to Bayard Street anymore I am sorry to say. Still, there is nothing like hoping for the best. If it never comes, we may have happy times in the new mansion.

My cold is all gone now. Am just as fine as can be and so is Ellen. I had a real bad week, the worst since I came here, but thank goodness, I am feeling splendid since. You are interested in me, Jim, to think of me so kindly, and you do know how I appreciate a few kind words from you.

I will wrap up warmly for the rest of the time here as I am out so much with the children, and won't it be lovely when we get to sunny south where all the beautiful flowers grow. What I would not give for you just to see the grounds of the Royal Palm!

The children have got to call you *Jim* now, talk about you. I often wish they would forget you 'specially when they ply me with questions regarding our relationship, right before the members of the family. Matthew often says, 'Well, Jim is not Annie's brother, and I know he is not her father. Then who is he?' But it's all right as long as you did not take me away, though they want to know when you are coming to the zoo with us again. They liked you well and they are dear little children. Many a happy hour they have given me. Jim, wouldn't there be a joke if we could talk over the phone? Just imagine how nice it would be to hear a dear voice again.

I am enclosing a few paper cutting[s] – quite interesting![2] I must finish up now, late as usual, and write me soon a long letter as I will still expect your uncle till I know he has left town.

Good night, and fondly I remain Annie. xxxxxx

The girls join me in wishing you a Happy and prosperous New Year.

1   Jim apparently sent Annie a framed photograph.
2   Annie enclosed a clipping that she dated 23 December [1902], entitled 'Street Car Men
Get $30,000 Award for Careful Work'. One of the sub-titles was 'Country Boys Do Well'.
The article described the premiums distributed to conductors and motormen by the
Pittsburgh Railways Company for a clean safety record for six months.

----

1 FEBRUARY 1903

4616 Bayard St. E.E.
Pittsburgh, Pa.
Feb. 1st 1903

My dear Jim,

How glad you all must have been to have your uncle home again,
but I was awfully sorry he couldn't have stayed longer for, really, I
cannot tell you how thoroughly I enjoyed his company. His nice
pleasant manner made me feel at home with him right away, and
how it pleased me to hear him talk so well of you, Jim. He is so jolly.
You cannot feel lonely while he is around. I am sure I wouldn't.

I got home just in time to see him. We were in New York since
the previous Thursday and got home on Tuesday which day he
called me on the phone, so I went to see him, and the nice evening
he showed me I cannot forget. He came all the way home with me,
but the girls had retired. You know I was so sorry to see him go
away, but I hope his trip here proved successful as then I may have
a chance of seeing him again.[1] He said your Aunt and Polly might
come to Pittsburgh sometime. Wouldn't I be glad to see them! I
wrote a few lines to Polly. I wonder if she received the letter.

Well, we are pretty busy now packing for our trip. We will leave
on the night of the 7th, and I suppose I'll not have another letter
from you to poor old Bayard St. though one before we leave would
be most acceptable and would cheer us on our long trip. Anyhow I
will be looking for one as soon as we get to the hotel and you may be

sure I will look for your pictures the first thing, and do let me keep one one if I get them.

We are not coming back to Bayard St. again. Poor old house where we had many a pleasant time. It seems hard to go to any other house now, but we will keep looking for the best. Everything will be moved into the new house while we are away, so that we can go right in on our return.

I do so wish, Jim, that you could only accompany us to that delightful south where it is always summer, but you can depend on me to write you often and tell you all about it. Rest assured that *more than one lone thought* will often stray away to you. Write to me often, for midst all the gaiety and gorgeousness of that place, a longing for the dear ones at home often steals upon us and makes us feel like being with them if it were only for a short time, but we cannot have everything we want in this life. I think Heaven has been real good to me, so I am perfectly happy.

I hope you will remember me very kindly to your Aunt and Uncle. I think I have right to appreciate their kindness as I certainly do.

You write me often and tell me all and do sometimes think a little of me. So now I remain with love

~~your own~~ fondly Annie xxxxx

*Florida address*   c/o W. L. Mellon
                Hotel Royal Palm
                Miami
                Florida
                Same as last
                year.
                Hotel Royal Palm

1   Jim's uncle Joseph Brennan did the tile work on the Bessemer Building. Conversation with Frank Phelan, 14 Nov. 2002.

---

2 MARCH 1903

[Envelope/paper of Hotel
Royal Palm, Miami, Florida]
Monday March 2nd

My dear Jim,

Your letter got here a few days after our arrival for we were twelve days on our boat having a lovely time and visiting some of the prettiest places in Florida. The boat is certainly fine, fitted with every modern convenience, electric light etc. and such a jolly time we had on board.[1] Maybe I didn't think of poor old *Adria*.

Then we got into the hotel in the evening midst all the splendour that wealth can provide. The folks went away again next morning, and we have not seen them since, but we hear from them quite often. They went south and are entertaining a party of Pittsburghers on their boat.

We are having quite a nice time here enjoying the beauties of this 'earthly paradise'.[2] No words could tell what a scene the Hotel and gardens present, but you can imagine yourself walking around midst beds of roses and surrounded by fruits of the rarest kind and sheltered from the scorching sun by those tall palmettoes whilst a delightful breeze is constantly blowing from the Ocean nearby.

We are having very hot weather now. The thermometer is near 90. I tell you we wouldn't mind having a little snow for a change, but the heat is not so much after 2 P.M. We have been on the river several times.

I lost no time in inquiring for *my* pictures, but they have no hope of ever getting them for me, so I put the matter in Mr. Merrill's hands and he will get them for me if he can. He is the Manager of the Hotel.[3]

Well, Jim, I was awfully disappointed at not being able to see your uncle. I just happened to go out that afternoon to say good-by to my friends, but I hope he will be in Pittsburgh when we get back.

I know Ellen would like to see him. She enjoyed the little talk they had over the 'phone and often speaks of him since.

I have expected an answer from Polly almost every day. Your uncle talked so much of her that I thought it would please him for me to write to her. He was so kind to me. She may write soon. It would be nice if she would come to Pittsburgh with her father. I guess I dare not ask you to come although I would like to. I only wish that our folks would take a turn and go west for a change. Then we would *all* see one another.

I wish, Jim, you would write me soon. Don't keep this very long as it takes four days to come here. I would have written this last night but went to Church. By the way, Ellen says to tell you the rudest people she has ever come in contact with inhabit this part of the country. They beat Pittsburgh for staring. They actually turn round on their bicycles to look at a person.

Well, dear Jim, must now finish and ask you once more to write soon and will answer yours sooner next time. With fondest love,

Annie xxxxxxx [4]

1    The first *Vagabondia* was a paddle-wheel steamboat. The German shipyard Krupp produced the last *Vagabondia* in 1928. It was 224 ft and carried a crew of 32 (Burton Hersh, *The Mellon Family: A Fortune in History* (New York, 1978), pp. 180, 245).

2    In 1900, *The Weekly Lake Worth News* described South Florida as an earthly paradise:

> To those wishing to enjoy life to its utmost,
>  in the most perfect climate on earth,
> midst the most beautiful environments
> we would say come to the Heaven-blessed land.
> Come once and the fascination will enthrall you.

*Palm Beach Post, Our Century: Featuring the Palm Beach Post 100* (New York, 2000), p. 3.

3    Henry Flagler recruited Henry W. Merrill from the Hotel Raymond in Pasedena, California (Edward N. Akin, *Flagler: Rockefeller Partner and Florida Baron* (Kent, OH, 1988), p. 145).

4    Annie enclosed a copy of the Hotel Royal Palm *Bulletin for Week Ending February 28, 1903.*

13 MARCH 1903?

> [Undated Postcard of the
> Hotel Royal Palm, Miami, Florida]

Dear Jim,
A Florida remembrance for the 17th.
    Annie x

---

19 MARCH 1903

> [Paper of the Hotel Royal Palm,
> Miami, Florida.]

My dear Jim,
I wish you were here tonight to listen to the beautiful music that is being played for a Japanese dancing affair held in the ballroom. I have just come up here and sent Ellen out. You know we must take turns as we both cannot leave our room, and I must say we have had a delightful time here and will be sorry when we must leave which will be on the 3rd April. Where we go after that is not yet decided, but I will let you know before we leave here.

We had a grand 17th, though I didn't have a speck of shamrock but had the pleasure of hearing some grand old Irish airs and seeing an Irish jig danced.

Senator Fairbanks' family are guests of Mrs. Mellon on her boat. They are from your city and gave me some *Indianapolis* papers to read which were quite a treat.[1]

I hope your uncle will not get through in Pittsburgh till I get back. We may get a little vacation as we always did.

A year ago I was looking for your picture and never gave up hopes of getting them till yesterday when I was told their whereabouts were not known 'were probably destroyed at the closing of the Royal Palm.' Now you see I must do without them. I would have given anything for the side face one. Some day I will *tell* you the reason why.

I hope the little book I sent reached you all right. When you have time, you will look over it and thus form an idea of the beauty of this region. The heat is growing more intense every day. I should not wonder if the north were beginning to thaw out now. I am glad for your sake as I know you like summer.

I have had many a dream of your visit, Jim, but they were only dreams. How far back on the horizon of the past does that week seem to be ~~I only wish~~ but you will come again *some day* and even that is something to look forward to for when pleasure reigns. There is a vacant place which none but *one* can fill. Well it is so late now I must hurry before they turn the lights out. *Be sure and write soon* that I may get it before 3rd April. Now remember me to all and give my kindest regards to your Aunt and Uncle. So, dear Jim, with my best love to you I now say good–night and remain as ever

Annie xxxxx

*special write very soon, Jim*

1    Charles Warren Fairbanks (1852–1918) was a United States Senator from Indiana, 1897–1905; he served as Vice-President of the United States during the Theodore Roosevelt administration (1905–9).

---

?APRIL 1903

On board the *Vagabondia*
[letter postmarked Stuart, Fl.]

My dear Jim,

We bade farewell to the Royal Palm when we got aboard our boat *Vagabondia* early on Friday last. We were very sorry for leaving that delightful spot where we had such a lovely time, but the longest day will always come to an end, and we are now steaming up the Indian River which is perfectly beautiful and interesting.[1] For miles it is so narrow that the trees on each side brush the boat and it requires a great deal of skill to guide a large boat like this through those narrow winding places, but we have a good captain and crew and I think we will get to Titusville (where we get the train for home) about the 14th and at that rate will be in Pittsburgh about the 17th.[2]

I will be looking for a letter from you as soon as we get home. I am anxious to know if your uncle will be there then. I hope he will as I *do* want to see him. I had a nice letter from Polly, but have not yet answered it.

I will be glad to get home again. It is nice to see someone you know. We have been among strangers so long. Rose wrote me some time ago. She asked most kindly for you and wishes to be remembered to you.

I am sorry we are not going to our old house. Instead we will stop at the Schenley Hotel for some time till our new house is ready to get in which may not be till June, so you will address your next letter to A. c/o W. L. Mellon, Hotel Schenley, Pittsburgh, Pa and don't forget, Jim. to write on the 14th.[3] I wish you were there to greet us. It will be nice to see your uncle again. It will be almost like talking to *you*.

The boat is rocking so I can hardly write, but I am not sea sick. Only the billows of the big ocean can do that. We were one whole day on the ocean going south and maybe we were not sick. All but Ellen. She is a fine sailor, but if she was on the *Adria* once, I bet she would be sick and scared too.

We are having a fine time and a delightful trip seeing some curious sights. I think I must now finish. We are getting to port and must mail this. I wish you a happy and joyous Easter, and do think of me. I don't know where we will be on Easter Sunday. Don't forget to write to me soon. Ellen sends her kindest regards, and I now must say a fond good-bye and remain your fond Annie xxx

1    Stuart, Florida is located at the junction of the Lucy River and the Indian River. The Indian River is a lagoon that opens to the ocean at many spots. (*The WPA Guide to Florida* (New York, 1984 [1939]), p. 306.

2    Titusville is located at the head of the navigable part of the Indian River.

3    Schenley Park, in the Oakland section of Pittsburgh, was the city's first public park. The site was the gift of Mary Schenley who donated 300 acres to the city.

———

29 APRIL 1903

[Hotel Schenley stationery<br>Pittsburgh, Pa.]<br>April 29th 1903

My dear Jim,

Back in the smoky city once more trying to feel 'at home' in our new quarters, a pretty hard thing to do when I pass by poor old Bayard St. every morning on my way to school. It is true that I miss the old house where we had many pleasant days and the memories connected with it shall not be forgotten by me. No one knows why I look so eagerly at the windows of the corner house room but *you* may guess. Yet let us hope bright days are coming.

The weather since we came here has been perfect – all but one day when there was such a fog you couldn't discern your best friend a square off.

I know by this time your uncle will have told you I called him up just as soon as I got here. You don't know what a pleasure it was to me to see him again. He is one of the nicest men I know, and I don't blame you for liking him so well. You may rest assured for you he has a particular regard. He is always ready to say nice things about you and in fact of the whole family.

He is leaving here soon, but I hope to see him before he does. It is too bad that I can do nothing for him. No one feels it more than I do to have done nothing in appreciation for his kindness. I am glad he has met with success here.

Well, Jim, if you could see our city now, really, I think you would like it. How I wish your dream would come true. It would be a pleasant surprise for me. I am glad to think that in your dreams you had my true nature. It is not the clothes, Jim, but you.

I expect we will be in Pittsburgh this summer or at least the greater part of it. I hope to get a vacation very soon and wish you were here to enjoy it with me, but otherwise it will be a little rest. Rose will take my place while she is doing nothing now. It will be a good chance for me to get away. You see they can not get into the new house. The girls are paid full wages and are staying with friends. Rose asked very kindly for you. She has been here a few times since we came home.[1]

Enclosed is a small medal given to me by our dear old priest in Miami the day I went to see him just before leaving. He gave me one for myself and one for my friend. I give it to you, and what sweet tokens they are of his great piety. Always keep it with you and no one need know about it.

Well, I do think I must now finish and Ellen wishes to be very kindly remembered to you. My kindest regards to all and please, Jim, do write soon if it is ever so short.

I remain

fondly Annie

---

1    Rose was Rose Werner, the Pennsylvania-born daughter of German parents. She is listed among the Mellon maids in the 1901 Census.

24 MAY 1903

[Hotel Schenley stationery
Pittsburgh, Pa]
May 24, 1903

My dear Jim,

I meant to have written ere this, but last week was a rather hard one for me. I was very sick for a day or two but not in bed though I tried to keep up and with Ellen's assistance pulled through all right. But really I did think I was in for quite a sick spell, but I am better now.

Your uncle came to see us, and maybe it wasn't a treat to have him again so pleasantly the time passes when he is around. I am sure you all miss him. If he only had you come with him. Yet, wasn't it nice to hear good reports from a city so interesting?

Sometimes I get awfully lonely and wish you were here, and again I keep looking for that *great future*. Your letters always bring a ray of sunshine. All things are guided by Heaven, so I hope ours are. Your uncle said you were coming this summer, but I think he was only teasing me. My, but I would anxiously watch that train coming in! Even that would be something to look forward to. I shouldn't be surprised if Polly took a trip here by this time. Jim, I am acquainted with them all in my mind, poor me.

This week is about the hottest I have ever known. Many deaths are the result, and so far there is not much relief in sight. We had quite a storm this morning, but it didn't seem to affect the temperature so much.

We were up at the new house yesterday and it is grand and in a fair way to let us in soon. I will be glad to get away from this hotel. It is so close and hot and no room to run around much. Give me a house any day in preference to the best hotel. You can have some little pleasure in a private house no matter how poor, but none whatsoever in a huge hotel like this where you have Sunday manners all the time. Sometimes I feel like going over to Schenley Park and giving vent to my lungs in a good hearty laugh.

I wonder how you are doing with my book.[1] I hope you will be successful, as I would be glad to help our poor old church that holds so many dear memories for me. I have such a longing lately for going home that it would not surprise me if I should go even for a very short time, just long enough to see all those old dear friends. The summer months would be the most delightful to be there. Ireland in the summer! What can equal it? All the places which I have visited were certainly beautiful, but none can boast of the music of the cuckoo's note. In fact, Ireland has qualities of her own never to be equalled.

Jim, you must write often to your uncle now that he is here again. I know he likes a letter from you as he often expressed that wish. And please, Jim, do write soon to me and why allude to making another happy. I am afraid you will be the one to take some fair lady by your side and forget all about me. Even if you did, Jim, I would always like you. Anyhow, don't be afraid of me. I am true to the last and it would be something terrible that should break my trust in you. You have the best love my heart can give, Jim, so rest assured and always remember me. Well, I am pretty tired now so must finish and do answer soon. I remain

    fondly Annie

    xxxxxxxx

---

1   Father Marcus Conroy must have sent some sort of pledge book for the St Éanna building project.

---

12 JUNE 1903

[Darlington Road & Forbes St.
Pittsburgh, Pa.]
June 12, 1903

My dear Jim,

This is the first chance I have had of writing since we moved in to this mansion, and fearing it might be some time before another would present itself, I take the advantage and try to tell you my little troubles. Our dread of this house long before it was built was certainly a foreboding of the reality. For the past few years, Ellen and I had the most pleasant happy times inseparable in all things and sister-like in our doings. Now that is a thing of the past as this house makes extra work thus calling me away from Ellen. Even the little room I call my own is no longer next to hers but on the next floor above. These are only little things, but so long as they leave us under the same roof I am satisfied.

One fine day French nurses will be taking our place as they have already a representative of every nation. Just imagine Irish, English, Scotch, Welsh, Swiss, Swede, German and *Japanese* are already employed, and a few more will be here ere long. The housekeeper is English, appears so far very nice and such a beautiful house as this is. But the poor old house will always be the dearer to me. The only nice thing about this is all our old girls are here, Rose and Mary, and of course that is everything. There is no possible chance of me forgetting you if I wanted to while Mary is around.[1] She reminds me of you every time she gets a chance.

The workmen are still busy here, and such a muddle as we came into, it will not be quite finished in another month. Well, Jim, I think I have seen Florida and Spring Lake with these people for the last time. They will remain here all summer and further than that, I don't know their plans. How glad I was to see your letter, a probability of your coming to Pittsburgh to stay. Won't it be nice when

I can see you. You say this will be the last summer we will be so far
apart. If that is so, I don't mind how quickly it may go. You will
surely find lots of work here, Jim, and then you see you will get to
like this city in time. If I only knew when you were coming, how
gladly I would look forward to the day.

Well, about going to Ireland. If I am spared till June of next year,
I will go, if only for a few weeks, and perhaps you would be able to
come then. I don't care to go any sooner and the summer months
are the nicest to be there.

Your uncle and I went to see Mrs. Connors, and they asked for
you very kindly. I did notice, Jim, that the old man does not look
well at all. In fact I made the remark to Ellen, but he works very
steady and then being away from the comforts of his nice home.
Now, Jim, don't let that interfere with your coming as Pittsburgh is
not so bad after all.

When you once get to work, you will really like it, and if I can
help you in any way, you know it will be a pleasure to me. Write me
soon and tell me everything as you know I am anxious to know all
about you. Won't I be glad when I don't have to write everything I
wish to say. I suppose it will yet be some time ere I can do that as you
will probably be stretching the time till you come here. I know you
have no love for Pittsburgh; however, I will still wait and some day
I *may* be rewarded. So now dear Jim, *won't you please write me very
soon*. I remain as
  ever Annie x

  Address –
  Annie O'Donnell
  c/o W. L. Mellon
  Darlington Road & Forbes Street
  Pittsburgh, Pa

1 This suggests that Mary returned to the household after the Mellons had moved to Ben Elm.

---

17 JULY 1903
[Darlington Road & Forbes Street
Pittsburgh, Pa.]
July 17, 1903

My dear Jim,

I was very pleased with your efforts in raising so much money for our church; indeed, I think you did well. I now have very near 45 dollars and that will be a help. Some of these days when I get out I will send it home.

Well, I know your uncle is now with you, and I am sure you will be glad. He called here just a day or two before leaving. He told me he had a letter from you and seemed so pleased with hearing from you. He seems quite anxious that you would try doing something here with him. Don't mention it, Jim, if he doesn't tell you, but of course if you get a better position at the barn, it may be better.

Well, maybe I didn't have a time watching for your last letter. Really, I thought you had forgotten me. Now make up for it this time and don't take so long.

We had quite a pleasant 4th in our new home. Had a grand view of the fire works in the Park, but the sorrowful 5th had its own tale.[1] Quite a number of homes were made lonely and sad. One poor motorman was killed instantly and three of his passengers by his car jumping over quite a precipice. The day ended in a dreadful thunderstorm causing the death of four persons.

My, but we are having torrid weather now! Just too hot to do anything. Now we miss the ocean breezes, and I think there are none in view for us. I am glad, in a way, to be in Pittsburgh some time. I will have a chance to get acquainted with it. But we will spend some time in the mountains. As yet I don't know when.

We really have a beautiful place here, and so far it is nice and serene. Everybody is pretty nice. Even the Jap, poor fellow, gave me a dollar for the Church. Do you know he likes your uncle so much. He was so sorry he was very busy the last evening he was here. Couldn't get talking to him at all.

Well now, Jim, I am about the latest up in the house, every one having retired, so I must finish too. Don't keep this so very long before you answer.

This would be elegant weather for a vacation in Ireland. I think it would be fun if we should happen the take the same steamer going there. We would have a nice time I know. I hope it will not be so very long till I can go, and then I will have one of the dearest wishes to see my parents and house once more. These few slips you will read when you get time so now must finish and *do please, Jim, write soon.* So with love

I remain

fondly Annie[2]

xxxxxxx

---

1    There were fireworks in Schenley Park on 4 July that included sky rockets and 'a set piece of Niagara Falls flowing in showers of golden sparks'. Ethel Spencer, *The Spencers of Amberson Avenue: A Turn-of-the-Century Memoir* (Pittsburgh, 1983), pp. 112–13.

2    Annie enclosed a description of the Spiddal church in 'Hiberno-Romanesque Revival' from the *Evening Telegraph*, 30 May 1903, and a newspaper cutting from a column called 'Poems You Should Know' from an unidentified newspaper. The poem 'Trouble-Proof' by Edwin L. Sabin appeared in the June number of *Lippencott's*:

> Never rains where Jim is –
> People kickin' whinin'
> He goes round insistin'–
> 'Sun is almost shinin!'
>
> Never's hot where Jim is –
> When the town is sweatin'
> He jes' sets and answers –
> Well, I ain't a frettin'

Never's cold where Jim is –
None of us misdoubt it,
Seein' we're nigh frozen!
He 'aint thought about it!'

Things that tie up others seem to
Never strike it!
'Trouble-proof,' I call it –
Wisht that I was like him!

---

5 AUGUST 1903
[Darlington Avenue & Forbes Street
Pittsburgh, Pa.]
August 5, 1903

My dear Jim,

We have just come home after spending a grand time in the country. I don't know when I saw the country look so beautiful and how I enjoyed farm life. I went back to old days once again, and I was glad to have an opportunity. The children's grandparents have one of the finest farms I have ever seen and in the prettiest location right in the heart of the Alleghany Mountains where, you remember, we stayed on our way home from the seashore each year.

Well, Jim, this is about the date I answered your letter some three [*sic*] Augusts ago. I bet you never remembered the 20th of July, but I did all that day. I didn't forget it once. That was the day you wrote your first letter to me, and about this time last year, Jim, wasn't I anxious for your coming. How time slips by. It doesn't seem any length since you were here, but I wish you were coming again.

I am so tired I can hardly see to write, so you will excuse all mistakes. I had quite a pleasant evening with your uncle. We talked about you *just a little*. I do really think, Jim, you are his favourite, but one of these days I will be sending *Carrie Nation* after you for smoking like she got after a young fellow here.

I had a letter from home today and just think I will soon get my father and mother's pictures. They have had them taken after my pleading for them these two years. You see 'all things come to him who waits' (*sometimes*).

They are all looking for me home next year, but they might be disappointed, for as yet I have not fully made up my mind. It depends entirely on my staying with the Mellons. By leaving here, it would upset all my plans, so let us hope they will keep me for at least another year.

I am getting awfully stout. Just think a few weeks ago I tipped the scale at *112*. Wasn't that enormous? I used to be 125. Well I knew I was getting so thin, but I nearly fell off the scale when I saw what weight I really was. You should be the one to lose. Poor me, I didn't have so very much to spare.

Well good night, Jim, I am so tired.

As ever Annie xxxx

---

20 AUGUST 1903
[Darlington Avenue and Forbes Street
Pittsburgh, Pa.]
Thursday 20th, 1903

My dear Jim,

Your letter reached me this morning. I got my parents' pictures. I am sending you one just to see what the poor bodies look like, but of course you will return it as soon as you can as I want to have some copies taken from it and have one enlarged. You will show it to your aunt. I know she would like to see it.

I have waited a long time for that picture, but it made my heart ache when I saw the difference that a few short years has made, yet, I must not be complaining when I think of their advanced age.

Nevertheless, I can never look at those dear faces without silently shedding a tear.

Mr. and Mrs. Mellon are away and we are having a jolly old time. You ought to be here now among this crowd of mischief makers. We never know what it is to have a serious look. There are all kinds of tricks played. I have just sewed up the sleeves of their nightgowns and the bed covers so that they can go so far and no farther. I put pepper in the pillows. You should have heard the sneezing. The funny part is when no one knows who is doing those things. My stock of mischief is now nearly worn out.

We had Mr. and Mrs. Connor here last Sunday, and when they were going home in the evening, we all went to see them off in the car. Jut as they got in, we threw handfuls of rice after them. You should have seen all the people looking at them thinking they were bride and groom. All the girls are crazy to get a chance of throwing some at me, and Rose and Ellen declare that if *you* ever come, there will be lots of rice on the car track. You know I would rather walk a mile to a street car than be caught.

I am glad to say we are having a real good time. We all expect your uncle out here tomorrow evening. I was talking over the phone last evening with him. He had your letter. I hadn't seen him since we came home.

My sisters and all the folks here are quite well. Mary's husband is fine now. They were very much worried for a few days but he got well real quick.

I hope you will be successful this winter if you should try to better yourself. Well now, I must finish as I hear the girls coming, so hoping to hear from you real soon.

I remain
fondly as ever
Annie xxxxx

10 SEPTEMBER 1903

[Darlington Road & Forbes Street
Pittsburgh, Pa.]
September 10th

My dear Jim,

I am sorry to have kept this letter so long, but I have been kept busy this week owing to a new nephew I got.[1] I went in to see my sister Mary almost every evening. She has a dear sweet boy. He is not yet christened, but I am almost sure his name will be William, our great family name. I am glad to say that Mary's husband is well again. It would have been terrible if anything occurred to him at such a critical time. They have a nice little family, two boys and one girl. I have one favourite, and I certainly do like him. He is the eldest, will be eleven in October, and his name is James. On my Sundays off I usually take him with me walking.[2]

Well, we had a jolly time here last Sunday evening when your uncle came and spent that evening with us. Indeed, I must say that he is well-liked here. When you come, you can look for a pleasant time, and, Jim, couldn't you steal away just for a short time? Really, you might stay with us altogether. Perhaps we would treat you nicer now.

That last contract your uncle got was quite a large one and seems as though he is to be in Pittsburgh for some time to come.[3] I don't think he is quite as stout now as he has been. I have not heard from Polly yet.

Well, I am glad you liked my parents' pictures, and I do hope that you will see them *there*. You would really like them, and if you ever go to Ireland, you certainly must visit Galway, and if I should happen to be there, you rest assured we would have a good time for there are so many nice places. Don't you hope that some day fortune will favour us and bring us together in that dear old Isle? It is pretty near five years since we left there, and yet, it doesn't seem that long.

Well, Jim, I am almost sure now that you will not answer this very soon, but really, Jim, I could not have written much sooner, so you write the first chance you get as I will be looking for it by *this day week* anyhow. If you see your way to come here, I sincerely wish you would come, but, of course, you know best. Now must finish and this is an extra long one. I want you to write a long one too. Remember me to all.

Fondly as ever, Annie

xxxxxxxxxxx

1    Eileen Phelan (Sr M. Gabriel) notes that Mary and Patrick Keady's son William was born on 29 August 1903.
2    Bridget's son James, born in 1892, was 11 in 1903.
3    This may have been the Bessemer tile job.

---

27 SEPTEMBER 1903
[Darlington Avenue and Forbes Street
Pittsburgh, Pa.]
Sunday 27, 1903

My dear Jim,
It is very nearly a year ago since that evening at the Union Depot. Yes, on Tuesday evening next.[1] That year passed away very quickly, and I do wonder if it will be still another year before you will come again. This time last year how anxiously I waited for that tram to come in, but this year there is nothing to look forward to but your letters which I wish would come oftener.

I don't suppose there is any chance of you coming before Xmas, but I think you would do all right here. There is no reason why you shouldn't. If I were you, I would come while your uncle is here. You don't know what you might happen to strike, but of course you know best, and in time everything will be all right. You know there is no one today wishes to see you more than I do. I won't hesitate to say it. If you see any chance for coming, just take it right away.

This afternoon we expect your uncle and Mr. and Mrs. Connor. Won't we have a good time. The Mellons are away. We had a very pleasant evening with your uncle two weeks ago, and I know he enjoyed it. Then, Mrs. Connor invited us for the whole day last Sunday. Your uncle and I went over there and maybe we didn't enjoy it. The Connors have the greatest respect for ~~Mr. Brennan~~ for your uncle and never tire of his company.

I had the nicest letter from Fr. Conroy a few days ago. It was such a nice one thanking all for their generosity towards his Church, and he promised to send me a prayer book, an Irish–English one.[2] I am looking for it now any day, and if you are good, some day I will let you read it, that is, when you master the Irish without making any mistakes like that awful one on the *Adria*.

Well, now I must finish before the folks come, as I would feel sorry for the rest of this letter if your uncle and Mr. Connor were near. I am tease-proof by this time though. No use in teasing me now. The only thing that bothers me is when they say, 'He is taking his best girl out now,' but I know different.

Ellen and I went in to see my sisters a few evenings ago. They are getting along so well, and the little baby is fine. I had the two big boys here all day yesterday and left them home last night on my way to Church.

While now my news is nearly exhausted so must finish, and do, Jim, write soon, won't you, and do come if you possibly can.

I remain, Jim

Your fondest Annie


P.S. Do write soon

1  The date suggests that Jim arrived on his visit to Annie on 29 September 1902, though other evidence suggests he arrived the day before.

2  There doesn't seem to be any record of Fr Conroy actually sending the prayerbook.

---

11 OCTOBER 1903
[Darlington Road and Forbes Street
Pittsburgh, Pa.]
Sunday night

My dear Jim,

I am all alone tonight and was just thinking of you so will write as I might not get a chance again for a few days as I am quite busy now sewing.

Well, I see you got one of those pictures. I certainly didn't think you were going to. That was got up as a surprise as we only got six altogether. Ellen proposed getting them to send Mother, so I see you got one as a surprise too. I am glad you liked them and Mrs. B. also. She must be real nice, Jim. You are so fond of her. I haven't seen your Uncle for more than a week, but I hope to before he leaves for home. Just think, I was in Indianapolis a few nights ago, and was I anxiously waiting for you in your uncle's house when at last I saw you coming up stairs. I called, 'Hello Jim.' Then the littlest Mellon called, 'Annie,' so I had to wake up. Wasn't that mean? You see when I happen to have a pleasant dream, I am rudely awakened, and last night no one would waken me when I had such a mean one. It wasn't about you though. I was in Galway last night.

You know, I think your Uncle doesn't look so well lately. It seems to me he has gotten much thinner. I don't think he would give up his city for this. Of course, in one way, I don't blame him. It is much cleaner, but this is a better one where money is concerned though again the expenses are high accordingly. I don't want him to discourage you, Jim, about coming, that is if he will, because you can only try it. I do believe you will easily do as well as away out west where you are, but I wish you would come soon. Why don't you come back this time with your uncle? Then you would have a chance of being settled before the winter. I know you could get on the streetcar here as a motorman. Then I would be happy, but I am afraid you won't come so soon.

Well, now, Jim, write soon. Even a short letter will be acceptable as long as you *just write soon*. So remember me very kindly to your aunt. And with best love Jim, I am

as ever Annie xxx

———————

28 OCTOBER 1903
[Darlington Road & Forbes Street
Pittsburgh, Pa.]
October 28th 1903
October 28th 1898

5

Write soon even
if its only a few
lines

My dear Jim,

Five years ago tonight I guess you remember.[1] Don't you wish we were on that same old spot but homeward bound? Your ever welcome letter reached me in good time and brought hopes of possible visit from you in a shorter time than I have anticipated. In fact, I have never fixed any time for your coming, but if it were depended on me, you would be here now. No matter when you come, it will seem long to me, and now I am beginning to look forward to your coming again. Then I'll be happy, for there are many things I would like to tell you that I can't write, and, Jim, I am very grateful to you for promising me your picture. It was something I always longed for but for which I will be looking now any day.

Our city is in quite a little distress these times, and the poor workmen are looking for a very slack winter.[2] Just a week ago, two banks closed and in all the mills and large works quite a number of the men are laid off, and to crown all, the whole city of Alleghany will be quarantined tomorrow morning on account of smallpox. I think that's dreadful! Mrs. Mellon is talking of having us vaccinated. I guess I remember when I was done last, but as usual, there is very little left to tell the tale, hardly a trace of that very sore arm.

When I was going to town a few days ago, our car came to one of those 10 minute stops, and the motorman came into the car and picked from his pocket a letter, started to read it, and such a bright face and hearty laugh. No one seemed to see but myself, for it brought to mind something similar in another city where a motorman opens a letter, but I fear not much room for laughter between the lines as the letters are rather dull at times.

Well, it is nearing Xmas again and our people are beginning to talk of the South already. That seems as important to them as the great day itself. Of course, they usually have to make purchases while the summer goods are on hand. Rose tells me to give you her best love and so does Ellen. They have told me often, but I guess I have to do it this time though I have asked them to wait till you come. They are the two best souls to me and think nothing too good to say about you and often wish you were here.

Now, Jim, please write soon and remember me to all so now must finish. I am as ever

fondly Annie xxxxx[3]

1   It was five years since Annie and Jim left Cork, and five years since they first met.
2   The 1903 Crash brought crises in the steel and coal industries (Hersh, *Mellon Family*, pp. 101–2).
3   Clipping included: 'James Whitcomb Riley Delights Large Audience. Hoosier Poet Delivers What May Prove to Be His Last Lecture in Pittsburgh.'

4? DECEMBER 1903

[Darlington Road and Forbes Street
Pittsburgh, Pa.]

(*excuse haste*)

My dear Jim,

Your letter reached me this morning and maybe I didn't look for it long enough. Really I thought all sorts of things and each time the mailman came only to disappoint me, so on Tuesday night I gave full vent to my feelings when all were asleep. I was awake thinking of a thousand things and found relief only in tears. I knew there was something beyond the ordinary or you would have written.

Well, of all things, I cannot imagine *you* in a saloon. What ever possessed you to think of one? I can picture you in almost any occupation but never behind a bar. I know it is a very *good* business, and I hope it will turn out so for you. I know I can trust you just the same. You are the same Jim to me no matter where you are. You do right, and then all things else will follow. You know, I am always ready to help you rather than discourage because you know what's best. The one thing that bothers me is that you are so far away and the length of time till I can see you. I wish luck would come our way just once, but it seems as though time was making your coming still further off.

I would like to go to Indianapolis, but that's an impossibility while I am with the Mellons, and I would like to stay with them as long as I can. We got orders today to prepare for Florida on 20th January. Just think of that and, Jim, you say you will come to see me when the roses bloom (which in *Pittsburgh is early in April*). That is something to look forward to.

Well, times are about the same here. Nothing exciting. Everyone is talking of Xmas, and the snow is fine giving a *clean* look to our city if that can be possible. I think it is the dirtiest place on earth on a rainy day, so you see we appreciate cleanliness when we see it.

I told Ellen and Rose what you were doing, and indeed they both gave you credit for trying to get along, but I am so anxious to know all about you and how well you do. Remember me sometimes and don't keep me waiting so long, for just a few lines help to cheer and make me happy. Now must finish for this time only wishing you were near.

Jim, you should write to your uncle. I haven't seen him in some time, as I was kept right busy. I wonder what he will say about your new step, but don't let anyone annoy you. You know best.

I remain dear Jim

fondly Annie

   xxxxxx

This time I want you to write very soon

---

22 DECEMBER 1903
[Darlington Road stationery]
December 22nd, 1903

My dear Jim,

I have been looking for an answer to my last letter for so long but can't imagine what prevented you from writing. I was so anxious to know how you were doing but finally came to the conclusion that something is wrong surely. I am afraid you are sick or you would never keep me waiting this long, but I sincerely hope tomorrow will bring a few lines from you.

We are all well and so busy preparing for our great day. It is the one time of the whole year that I love, and everything I can do to make the little ones happy is my delight. We certainly have a fine mansion this year to receive Santa and three dear little children waiting for him. It gives lots of work and keeps us up very late, but happiness is greater than all.

Well, Jim, I gave your uncle a little parcel for you which he will give probably on Thursday night, or I think you will find it in your room as a surprise. It is mean of me to tell it, but I have to. Understand the circumstances. There is a small package marked 'Mr. Brennan' which you will give him. It's a white muffler I made for him, and, Jim, the *red* one I made you just at the time you had about left the streetcar. I thought it would be good and warm to put around your neck when going out those cold days, but I am sorry now it is not a *white* one. I am sure you would like it better, but I think you will like the *glass*, and for a long time I have thought of getting you one.

*I know men are so particular about shaving.* Your uncle was trying to joke me about it, but I told him 'You would have it hanging in your room as soon as you got it.' I wish you would see what he would say, but don't let on I said anything about it.

Well, Jim, your Christmas can not be any brighter than I wish, as you have the best wishes my heart can afford. The one thing that would make my Xmas brightest would be a 'shake hands' from you, but my prayer is still the same – that this will be the last Christmas you will be *so very far away*.

Now I want you to wish Mrs. B and all the family a 'very happy Xmas' from me, and just give one one lone thought towards old smoky Pittsburgh when you are enjoying yourself with your friends. All the girls join in best wishes to you.

With my best love, Jim

I remain Annie. xxxxxxxx

xxxxx

---

28 DECEMBER 1903

[Darlington Road & Forbes St.
Pittsburgh, Pa.]

My dear Jim,

'Many thanks' for your very nice gift is all I can say, but if I could express my thoughts sufficiently, it would give you at least a *little* idea of the pleasure you gave me on Christmas Day. The ring is awfully pretty, Jim, and I wouldn't have it exchanged for the world, but how you guessed my size is something I cannot understand. It fits just as though you had taken my measure. You would be actually surprised if you could but see how nicely it fits. I was in such haste to wear it that on Xmas morning I got up at 3: 30 and put it on. Then we got ready and went to early mass at the cathedral. It was a Pontifical High Mass and most beautiful.

It was a decided white Xmas. Till about 4 in the afternoon it was like a June day when suddenly the thermometer dropped and before 8 PM there was a foot of snow. Since then we have been having zero weather, but today is the worst of all. We are nearly snowed in. I had an awful time going to and coming from Church, so I decided to stay home for the rest of the day and look over my treasures which all my friends gave me for Xmas. Before doing so, I want to write you which to me is the greatest pleasure. I think it was so nice of Polly to have remembered me. I am sure you all had a good time if your Uncle was home.

Mrs. Mellon and the children as usual remembered us, but this year more generously than ever (a nice cheque and from the children, some very useful things). Ellen, Rose, Mary and Mrs. Walters' gifts were really too much, so I can not thank them enough. Some day when you will see them, Jim, you certainly will think I have a few nice friends. Their gifts I cannot wear, but some day they will be very useful. I got so many nice things. I just can't tell you all, and thanks to my friends, I had the happiest Xmas Day of any since I came to Pittsburgh. I only hope yours was equally so. Oh, how often during that day did my thoughts stray to Indianapolis, and there is but one who can tell what those thoughts were. I felt quite bad about your trouble but am glad it was over then. I knew there was something wrong with you, and the dream I had, but, of course, I give no credit. I am not superstitious in any thing. There is only one thing I do believe, and I believe it firmly, 'that what's to be, will be' in spite of all. I felt so worried, for I answered your letter the very day I got ours. Then I got no answer till the one you sent with the ring.

I do want to know if you got your things in good time and how you liked them. Of course, I expect a letter very soon and give a little account of how you are doing in the *Saloon*. Jim, I have one request to ask you and wonder if you will grant it. It is one that will bring more happiness to me than anything you could do for me. I hardly think you will refuse me, but anyhow I will consider it a favour and, in return, I will give you anything you ask considering it is within my reach. Now my request is *that you will write to me every Sunday* unless sickness or anything likely to prevent your doing so should occur. If you do that, Jim, it will be something I shall always thank you for.

Well, now hoping this long letter will not weary you, I must bring it to a close and hoping it will find you real well, I will finish and again thanking you for your nice gift and the happiness it brought with it. I remain, dear Jim

your fond Annie

xxxxxxxxxx

# *1904*

✦

[Darlington Road & Forbes St.
Pittsburgh, Pa.]
January 1, 1904

My dear Jim,

A bright, happy and a prosperous New Year is my sincerest wish to you. A few minutes ago I had a talk with your uncle over the phone. I was awfully glad to hear his voice again, but he told me you were not at all well, that you looked ill, and were, in fact, suffering from a severe cold. That's the reason I now write, for rest I cannot get till you yourself give me an accurate account of how you really are, if you have not already written. Our last letters must have crossed as we both wrote on the same day.

Wasn't it too bad you didn't come here during the Christmas week? Yet, it might have been for the best, as I never was more busy since I came to Mellons. Now they have decided not to go south till 30 January, and I wish they were not going at all. I feel too far from you now, but when I go to Florida, I just feel lost. Jim, if you are feeling ill, consult a doctor at once and, for pity sake, do be careful while this cold weather is here.

Your uncle said you were doing nicely *I said nothing* but listened to all he had to say, and, Jim, don't you worry about things. If the saloon does at all, well, just keep with it, and, of course, if you don't find it quite to your liking, I see no reason why you wouldn't get along with something else. Don't worry about what anybody says. Just suit yourself and you will come out all right. I would give the world tonight if I were near you to give at least a few encouraging words. As you left me at the Union Station, so I have been since. Always remember that no matter what comes or goes, I will *always* be the same. In your troubles, Jim, you will find in me an ardent heart, and don't think you will worry me by telling me as there is no greater happiness for me than to help you.

Now tonight I beg of you to answer this as soon as you get it, and just let me know exactly how you are as I may be fretting for nothing. I assure you I have felt quite anxious since I talked with your uncle. I am going to see him as soon as I can, and I do hope you will write to me so very soon.

Jim, everybody likes my ring. Mrs. Mellon saw it today for the first time. She liked it but said she hoped it meant nothing till her children grew bigger. Then she could trust them to a stranger. I kept silent.

Now, good night, dear Jim and hoping heaven will bless the future, I remain, your fondest Annie xxxx

---

11 JANUARY 1904
[Darlington Road & Forbes Street
Pittsburgh, Pa.]
Monday night

My dear Jim,

I meant to have written last night, but it was so late when I got home that I was obliged to put it off till now though it is quite late. I went to the station on Saturday night to meet Pollie.[1] I made it a point to be there when she came in. Your uncle, of course, was with me. Then yesterday I was free all day (which will be the only free one

I'll have till we go south). I spent the day with her and in the evening we went to see Mrs. Sietz, her friend from Indianapolis, and tomorrow she will come out here and spend the day with me. Her father will come towards evening.

I like her very much, Jim, and the only thing I am sorry for is that she cannot be with me more or ~~at least~~ that I can't show her at least a little attention while she is here.

On occasions like this, I feel what it is to be working under a *boss*. Whilst my position is a very nice one, it is terrible confining, and it is a mean thing to be refused a few days vacation when a friend comes but once in a lifetime. Still, I must stop complaining as there are a few waiting to step into my place as soon as I would get out. The reason we are all so busy now is this southern trip and all its preparations as a few of our party will leave here on Monday next. We don't go till the 29th or 30th but no later.

There are so many places I want to take Pollie to, and, if I can possibly do so, I assure you it will be done. If the Mellons were away, what a good time we would have, but unfortunately, we have extra people instead who will go south with Mr. Mellon on Monday next.

I think she likes Pittsburgh, and, Jim, it was so nice to hear her talk about you. She assured me that you looked real well though not feeling quite up to the mark. Your uncle asked why she didn't coax you with her, but just think if you did, Jim, I couldn't even go out with you only two afternoons this week, and you couldn't see me till 9 at night. Don't you think that's awful mean? You cannot imagine how I feel about it.

Our baby has just recovered from an attack of pneumonia. Ellen and I took her every other night in succession and depended on two or three hours of sleep during that time. I think if we do not look out, we will be the next to have something like pneumonia.

I don't know when I felt so badly as I have been today, and poor Ellen received a message a few hours ago that a very dear friend of hers was so very ill. It was then quite late, but still she went out to see her, and I am waiting for her return.

Well, dear Jim, I am looking forward to your letter tomorrow, and I think it was very kind of you to comply with my wish, and, Jim, I will not forget it. How nice it is to know what place in your life I occupy whilst there are so many predictions among my friends here that you will soon forget me. My answer is, 'He may but I'll never forget him,' and that topic ends right there. These predictions have been going on now since that dear old letter found me at Spring Lake. They have not come true, and that sweet token you sent me is a protection to me now when such topics happen to arise. It takes a long time for people to know my nature, but once they know it, I think I gain favor with all.

Well, now I must bring [this letter] to a close and hope this will find you real well. I now remain with fond love.

as ever Annie. xxxxxxxx

1   Pollie Brennan was Jim's cousin.

---

18 JANUARY 1904
[Darlington Road & Forbes Street
Pittsburgh, Pa.]
Monday, Jan. 18th

My dear Jim,

Ere this reaches you, I am sure Pollie will have told you of her opinion of Smoky City as I think she will leave us tonight. Her visit I looked forward to with the greatest interest; yet, it seems like yesterday since she came, and now she is off again. She had supper with us last night. We expected your uncle too, but he couldn't come till quite late. Anyhow we had a pleasant evening. *You* were the subject we talked about principally. If she remembers all the messages that were sent to you from the girls, you will certainly say that you will have a cordial welcome on your return to our city.

I am going to see Pollie off at the station if I possibly can, and if not, I shall indeed be very much disappointed as you wish to be the last there to be the first remembered to you when she gets home. In my heart I wish I were going with her, but very soon we will be at that same station going on our southern trip, but that doesn't count.

All the girls like Pollie so much, and I must say she is a girl I could be very fond of. The more I knew her, the more I liked her and all the nice things she said about you. I only hope that she will find somethings equally nice to say about me, but I know she can't. She saw Mr. and Mrs. Mellon and the children. My little girl was quite anxious to know all about Jim. Said she wished he would come to see us soon.[1]

Well, Jim, when you come next time, are you going to stay here? I am almost sure you will as you will get to like Pittsburgh if you are here a little while.

I am now in such a hurry. You will excuse my mistakes. Must finish. There were so many things I had to say before Pollie came, and now that she is here, it seems they have all vanished. Anyhow, you can rest assured of my best love and hoping to have a longer letter next time must now say

good–bye and remain

fondly Annie xxxxxxxx

1  Rachel was almost five in January 1904. She was born on 16 February 1899.

20? JANUARY 1904

[Darlington Road & Forbes Street
Pittsburgh, Pa.]
Wednesday

My dear Jim,

Well, we saw Pollie off last night, and I assure you I didn't feel as gay as the evening I went there to meet her. I am not much when it comes to saying good-bye. Honestly, I felt sorry for your uncle. He is such a good old soul himself. I felt sorry to see her go for his sake. We stood just where you saw me last, and I waved to her as long as her train was in sight. As we turned towards home, well did my thoughts go back to that dreary morning when that same old train carried away my heart. On our way to the car your uncle kept calling my attention to furniture stores etc., but, at the same time I could see he missed Pollie and often did he say, 'She'll be telling Jim all about you for she told me that Annie was horrid and she didn't see why Jim ever cared for her.' You know he teases me terribly sometimes, but I take it all and have lots of fun. I know he likes me, or he wouldn't take the trouble of even teasing me.

We will have him out here one evening before we leave, and I expect to see him on Sunday if I can go out. Wasn't it too bad that Pollie couldn't have stayed a little longer? We had set Thursday evening for a visit to my sisters. All the girls were invited, and the housekeeper would see that we all got off. It was too bad they couldn't have been earlier in setting an evening for us, but I must not be too hard on them now, for my boy was not well and they had no idea that Pollie would leave so soon.

How disappointed they will be as no doubt they will have everything as nice as they can, and they are so sensitive about small things. I know they will feel bad. Ellen, Rose and I will go in and explain matters. Ellen is very fond of them and I am sure, Jim, *you* will have no trouble when you come here this time in gaining their affection. They are hard to get acquainted with, but once you know their little odd ways, there is nobody can be nicer. They are now 15 or 16 years here. and I don't believe they know half a dozen families.[1] They are real Irish in their thinking, and I believe America will never change them. Whenever Ellen or Rose go in, they claim they can't spend a more pleasant evening anywhere. And since they found that you are soon coming, they speak of you quite often. My sister Mary said, 'Just at Xmas time, I hope we will be in a nicer house and have a better chance of seeing him when he comes this time.'

How nice it is to think about your coming and really the time will not be so long after all. If you come when we get back, then you will stay, and I will be happy. There will be a few other anxious people looking for you too. If you only knew half of all the nice things that are said about you, Jim, really I think you would get vain.

I am awfully glad you joined that society. It is quite a thing here. Most of the young men here have joined it. I can imagine you laughing going through all those performances. I don't believe I'd ever get through, but I know they exaggerate a good deal, and it's only fun after all.

Well, Jim, indeed I often make that old mistake not only to Harry but to the Jap, but poor Jap will not be with us now very long, and he feels so bad about it. The Mellons want competent help. They pay good wages, but you must be just right, or you can go. It doesn't take long for them to tell you so.

George was so nice to us, and he thought the world of your uncle, and he always called you, 'Mr. Jim, when is he coming? I want to see him?' Whilst Pollie was here, the weather was pretty fair, but since she left, the rain has not ceased for a minute. The streets are flooded and an attempt at walking is impossible. Seldom have I heard of a girl spoken of so nicely, but Pollie is one of the nicest girls I have met. She has an attractive manner that endeared her to all and so jolly. How we all enjoyed the time she spent with us.

I have written this letter under difficulties, started it on Wednesday and this is Thursday evening, so you will excuse mistakes. I am so anxious to get your next letter. It will tell me all about Pollie's trip and what she thought of Smoky City. I know she was tired when she got home. Now, Jim, let Sunday's letter be a long one and give my love to your aunt and Pollie. I must now finish. With my best love to you, Jim, I am

as ever Annie

xxxxx

1   Bridget came to Pittsburgh in 1888, and Mary came in 1890.

---

20 JANUARY 1904
[Darlington Road & Forbes Street
Pittsburgh, Pa.]
Wednesday night

My dear Jim,

I have just come home after saying good-by to your uncle as this was my last evening off. Will leave on Saturday night. It is now very late and all have retired save poor me. If you only saw me trying to write these few lines fearing that at any moment the light would be turned off; yet, I want this to reach you before your next Sunday's letter.

Your uncle looked real nice and, well, judging from the amount of work he has now on hand, it may be some time before he can get home. He said he had a letter from you also from Pollie. She had her pictures taken here. I did think she would write to me ere this, but I suppose she was quite busy.

I always feel lonely when it comes time to leave. Dirty and smoky as poor Pittsburgh is, yet I have more nature for it than for Florida. Jim, about that muffler question, don't you believe it.

They were just trying one on me. Honestly, I never made but the two in my life (yours and the old man's). I assure you I must think an awful lot of a man before I sew anything for him. The one and only thing I am longing for in Florida, Jim, is your letters. They are the one thing that will help pass away the time and then the fact of knowing that it will be soon till we can once again talk and that you will stay here then. All this would be enough to make me happy, and I'll think of you always.

Perhaps Pollie had been telling you of a good one they tried on me, and I fixed it all right. They claimed you had a ladies' glove in your possession, just one glove as a keepsake. 'Oh,' I said, '*I* can easily account for that the mate of it is in *my* trunk.'

Well, Jim, a few days ago I was on the streetcar, and I am almost sure I saw 'Mayo Jim'. You remember the old lady's son, and really I felt like asking him about his mother, but I felt somewhat timid, so I let it pass. My thoughts went far back to the old *Adria* and the pleasant crowd, and I wonder if when crossing again should there be such another little jolly crowd.

There is one thing that would make me feel dreadful bad as now I would realize more fully the parting from my parents. I guess if I don't soon finish up, I'll be through all my saddest days. It seems as though tonight when I feel so blue, all my old lonely times come present. I wish I had a letter from you before I leave. When I get to Rockledge, there will be your nice one waiting for me. Next Sunday's letter address to me.

c/o W. L. Mellon
Rockledge P.O.
Rockledge, Florida

Boat *Vagabondia*

Then the following Sunday address it to:

Hotel Royal Palm
Miami
Florida

c/o W. L. Mellon
Be sure to have it always in care of W. L. Mellon.

Good-bye, as ever, Annie

———————

5 FEBRUARY 1904
[*Vagabondia* stationery]
[Palatka, Florida]
Wednesday night

My dear Jim,

We arrived at Rockledge late on Monday evening, and I would have written you sooner, but we are miles away from any P.O. and now are beginning to move a little nearer one, so you will probably get this letter before Sunday. Your letter hasn't reached me yet but hope by tomorrow evening to get it. I never felt so lonely leaving Pittsburgh as I did this time, and the girls certainly didn't make it much easier as they were in tears as we were leaving. Rose misses us more than anyone, and for a whole week before we left, she would sigh and say, 'I wish you were coming home instead of going.'

Well, I never had a harder or more tiresome trip than this one, and I was so glad to get off the train and get to our nice boat which was quite a pleasant change from the horrid old train. We were the poorest crowd you ever saw on Monday evening. [We] looked as though we had been seasick for a week, but a good wash and a little rest fixed us all up and are now enjoying the balmy breezes of this delightful country. The weather is beautiful, so warm and nice. Just too lovely for words. I wish you were here. You would be enraptured over the different scenes that present themselves.

We spent the greater part of today on the beach and in the afternoon went fishing, and tonight we are all so sunburned.[1] I like this kind of life that gives you freedom to enjoy nature in all its grandeur, and it always brings back those old days of precious memory when I roamed about the fields and gardens and felt no care, but there is a certain wildness about this place that I can never fancy. We were quite close today to what appeared to be 'a deserted village,' some 10 or 12 houses all in fair shape but not a creature within miles of them. It just looked as though all left at the same time. This is such good fishing ground. Our party have stayed a little longer, but once we move from here, we will lose no time in reaching Miami.

Don't forget to address your next letters to the Royal Palm Hotel, Miami, Fla. I'll be glad to get a word from anybody now. It seems like ages since I heard from you last, but once we get to Miami, there will be no trouble in getting our mail. Please, Jim, excuse this scribble tonight. It is merely to let you know I am still in the land of the living, though amidst the wilds of the Indian River, and that I do not forget you. Often when Ellen and I sit on deck, we talk of our friends. There is not one mentioned oftener than Jim.

The boat is a *little* bit rocky, so notice the difference in my writing, Hoping to have your letter by tomorrow. Remember me to all, and with my best love to you, dear Jim. I am your Annie

xxxxxx

1    W. L. Mellon was an enthusiastic sports fisherman.

---

16 FEBRUARY 1904

[Hotel Royal Palm stationery
Miami, Biscayne Bay, Florida[1]]
February 16, 1904

My dear Jim,

We got into Miami last night, and I did try hard to write you a few lines, but really I was too tired to even talk after I had gotten things in order for the night. Ellen said, 'Oh! Jim will excuse this time, Annie. Go to bed.' I hope you will, and I know it won't happen again.

Well, we did have a delightful time on the boat. The only thing was, we didn't get our mail till Wednesday last owing to the boat striking a sandbank. For a time I was really afraid we wouldn't be able to get to Miami. For some time the water in the river was so low. Both of your letters, Jim and Pollie's, reached me all right, and maybe I wasn't pleased to get them. Pollie's letter was so jolly. It certainly cheered me up a good deal. After all, mid all those pleasures and grand places still one letter from home and the dear ones is worth more than all put together.

Your nice letter was the first and only greeting I had on my arrival at the hotel. I was quite surprised at your uncle being home again. Still he travels around a good deal, so it makes it nice for him and you all that he can go home so often. I am anxious to know if you will come to Pittsburgh to stay. I have yet that dread that you will only come like you did last year – just for a short visit. Wouldn't it be nice if you stayed with us all the time and not have any mean parting like last time?

The little children remember just as well and talk of you oftener than anyone, but my little girl thinks it so funny that Jim wants Annie always when he comes. He could come, but just leave Annie with her. That's all she wants. You will see a big change in them. They have all grown so, and maybe they are not having a good time in Florida especially while on the boat. It was just the thing for them.[2] They were dressed in overall and gum boots, so you can form an idea of what they could do in that rig, but here they must have their ribbons and laces and I must say I feel proud of them as they do look well.

This place looks so pretty. There are just a few new additions, and everything helps to make it more attractive than ever. We are having very hot weather, but it seems almost unbearable parts of the day here and often do we wish for a little of the frost and snow you write of.

If I can get any picture of the boat, I will sent it as I would like you all to see it. I saw in one of the Florida papers an account of it, but nothing can speak too well of the comfort and home-like feeling it gives.

Mr. Mellon is now on his way to Pittsburgh and will not be back for two weeks or more, so Mrs. will entertain parties on her boat for just very short trips. We spent Sunday last at a place called Soldier Key, but I am glad to say we are near our own little church today.[3]

Well now, Jim, I will ask you to excuse me this time. Remember me very kindly to your Aunt and Pollie and the old man whenever you write to him. I will write to Pollie maybe tonight, so now must finish and will soon write you a long one. Now, Jim, believe me to ever remain, your fondest Annie xxxxx

Ellen wishes me to send you her kindest regards and to hurry and get ready for Pittsburgh.

1    Letter forwarded from 1719 North Senate Avenue, Indianapolis, Indiana to c/o Mr Joseph Brennan, Colonial Hotal, Pittsburgh, Pa.
2    'By 1901, they'd produced three "chicabiddies" – Matthew in his steel-rims, Rachel, Peg-urchins, barefooted in cheap straw hats scampering along the beaches with bags for shells, trolling with canepoles off W. L.'s old paddle-wheel steamboat, the original *Vagabondia*, fiddler crabs skipping behind the boat.' Hersh, *Mellon Family*, p. 182. See the photograph of Matthew and Rachel opposite p. 182.
3    Soldier Key is a coral reef on the northern edge of Biscayne National Park in Florida.

19 FEBRUARY 1904

[Miami, Florida]
Friday night
February 19, 1904

My dear Jim,

I really thought your last Sunday's letter would never reach me, and I knew you wrote, yet, I couldn't help thinking something was wrong, so last night at the very last mail 10 P.M., I went to the office and got it and read it on the way to my room. I won't tell you what I felt like the rest of the night, but I woke up wishing I was in Pittsburgh. I think that is the meanest thing I ever known. You in Pittsburgh and poor me away down here, but won't I be the pleased creature to know that you will be there when I get home, and how I wish the time would fly so we could see each other.

I will be so anxious to know just everything and what you will do. There is only one thing I ask you. Don't get discouraged, and, by the time we get back, you will have a good opinion of Smoky City. I know you will miss the nice home you have had and its pleasant surroundings, Mrs. B[rennan] especially, but then you could go back some times and see them all. Then you will have your uncle. He'll see that you will not get lonely. Then, Jim, when I get home, we will have some good times together.

I would say to call on Rose and Mary, but there are some new girls and I think they don't very well agree, so wait till we both be together and then it will be nice. But I would give anything for you to see Rose. She is my best friend in that house. I won't tell anyone you are there, but we'll surprise them one evening as soon as I get back. You don't know, Jim, how I feel to think that at last you are in Pittsburgh *to stay*.

Do write me a long letter telling me all, and I will be so anxious to know how you will be doing. I wrote Pollie a few nights ago and tell the old man I will soon write to him and I promised him I would, and I want you to remember me very kindly to him.

There is one thing I feel sorry about and that is the very few to greet you there, even a few lines from me. I guess you will have a few streetcar rides. It takes so long for a letter to come from here.

Well, we are all fine here, and I have gained steadily since I came down. The children are grand. We have met so many people, lots of them from Ireland, and only one from Galway, but she is too proud to claim any relationship with that grand country.

This has been the coolest day we have had since we came here, *only 72*. It was quite a little change from the scorching days we have had. I suppose you are all having lots of snow, but I think it is pretty near as nice as this real hot weather we've been having.

Now, Jim, I must finish for this time and will be so anxious to how how you will get along. Don't get lonely or discouraged, but cheer up and I know you will get along, and sometimes think of poor me among the Florida flowers and palms often seeking shelter under those trees and lonely listening to my own thoughts. It will take me some time to get acquainted with your new address. Now [I] have no more to say, only best wishes from Ellen and wishing you all good luck,

I remain,

Your fondest Annie xxxxxx

---

28 FEBRUARY 1904
[Stationery of Hotel Royal Palm,
Biscayne Bay, Florida[1]]
February 28, 1904

My dear Jim,

So you are really in Pittsburgh, and I am glad of it. Isn't it nice to think that you will be there and quite at home with the different places when I get back. You don't know how homesick your last letter made me and how I would have enjoyed the trip to Connors.

You know, I am quite surprised at you not getting my letters. I think it is so queer as I got every one of yours, but perhaps they have reached you by this time. I wonder if you are writing to me tonight or what you are doing. I hope you are not lonely, and I am glad you moved from the hotel, and won't I be glad when we get ready to leave this one.

Nearly every night when Ellen and I have done the work for the day and the little ones are in bed, we sit in my room and talk and maybe you are not often spoken of. Ellen and Mrs. Walters and Rose some time ago were sitting in the nursery in Pittsburgh and in some way you were mentioned, so they said if you ever came, what they wouldn't give to see us meet. Between your uncle and Mrs. W. and Ellen, it was often discussed, and I believe they would have gone to the Union Station unknown to me, but now we can have the joke on them. Ellen says she will write to Mrs. Walters, so they will fix it up between them, but ere we are through with Florida, you will be well-acquainted with our streets. I wonder if you will be any where near old Bayard St.

I hope the weather is getting milder now as it has been quite a severe winter. Talk about summer! Why, for the last four weeks we were right in it, and it is getting hotter every day. I am surprised there are not sunstroke cases. The natives claim sunstroke is unknown, but instead malaria is very prevalent in some parts, inland and near swampy places. We are out on the bay and get the good ocean breezes; yet, about noon, the heat is so intense that it is almost unbearable. Towards sundown it again cools off and in the evening it is beautiful.

We go for a walk along the beach every evening after supper with the children, and it is so glorious on a moonlight night. How you would enjoy it if you were here, and you can rest assured that you are not forgotten for whenever one thing pleases me, it is then I miss you most.

My little girl Rachel has taken quite a fancy to your picture since we came here. She and I sleep together, and the first thing in the morning she goes to the dresser and takes your picture and kisses it and then runs to me and cross-questions me. She says she really likes Jim, but he takes her Annie away. I told her *you* would see her very soon, and the dear little thing put her arms about me and said she likes her Annie better than anyone in the world.

Well now, dear Jim, I must finish up as things are about the same here and as usual I am wondering how you are getting along and if there is anything you would like me to get you here.

If you go to the Mellon house to see the girls, you ask Rose to show the picture of our boat as I am afraid I'll not be able to get any this year.

I suppose you went to the Sacred Heart Church today and wonder if you remember the day you and I knelt there together.[2] Don't forget to remember me very kindly to Mr. and Mrs. Reese and little George. By the way, you will see Jap as he wrote to Mrs. Mellon and said he couldn't get work, so I suppose he will stay on half pay till we return.

I wrote to your uncle today and will soon write to Rose and Mrs. Walters. I am glad you like her. She is real nice and writes the nicest letters. She tries to make the time pleasant for us if she can. Won't they have a lot to say when we get back. Write a long letter, Jim, and tell me how you are doing. So now with the fondest love, Jim

I remain as ever Annie xxxxxxx

P.S. Ellen wants me to tell you there are so many *attractive* girls in Pittsburgh that you must be careful not to notice any of them. She sends her kindest regards and best wishes.

1    Letter sent c/o Mr. J. Brennan, Colonial Hotel, Sixth Street, Pittsburgh. Printed on envelope of Hotel Royal Palm: H. W. Merrill, Manager

Where January
Is turned to June
And perfect days
Pass all too soon

2    Sacred Heart Church is located in Pittsburgh's Shadyside neighbourhood. It would
have been Annie's parish church when she lived at 4616 Bayard Street.

---

28 FEBRUARY 1904

[Hotel Royal Palm stationery
Biscayne Bay, Miami, Florida]
Sunday night[1]

My dear Jim,

I have just finished a letter to Pollie and may be the address wasn't
familiar, so now it is quite late and I cannot write you a very long one.
I am wondering where you are now. I hope you will have a chance of
going around to see different places. It will be so nice for you.

I was so glad to know you were going to Philadelphia. Perhaps
you would meet some of our old friends, but don't you stay there
long, and, above all, don't be out of Pittsburgh when we get there.
My! but that would be a disappointment after all my thinking since
I knew you had come.

We expect Mr. M [Mellon] on Wednesday next, so we can then
tell when we will leave here and also when we will arrive home. I
might write to you again before Sunday and let you know.

Well, I had the nicest letter from Rose, but I am not going to tell
you all the nice things she said about you. We had one from Mrs.
Connor too. She told us all about the joke on her.

Well, Jim, this place is fine. Nothing could be more beautiful,
but yet there are times when we feel lonely and now that a number
of people are leaving and the place will get quite a deserted look. We
wish that we too were leaving. We went around the rose garden a few
days ago. I picked a few, so I pressed them for you.[2] Now they don't

look much, but they were then lovely. I wore them all day and then pressed them; they are the loveliest things here, those grand roses.

I knew you would find Pittsburgh a good deal more expensive than Indianapolis. It is quite a hard city for a person with limited means to get along in. Everything is so very high. I am sure you find little George Reese quite a companion.[3] I think he is a dear little fellow. I did want his picture so hard, but I only went there once, and they were not finished then. He called me Mrs. Brennan.

It is a wonder Mrs. Walters didn't tell you. She always said she would, but then she didn't know how soon she was going to see you. It is too bad she will be leaving us for good in June, and I know we will never again get one so good. She wrote me and wanted to know how would I like a cup of tea with Jim, but wait till I get there I'll pay her back. I don't even have a cup of tea nor coffee down here, but won't it be nice when I can have one with you.

Well now, dear Jim, I must finish and will be anxiously looking for your letter, so *remember me sometimes* and give my kindest regards to all. Ellen sends her best; she doesn't say much but look out for some teasing when she sees you. You will remember me to your uncle. I hope he is well.

Now good night, Jim, and wishing you all kinds of good luck and accept my best love always, I remain

Your fondest Annie

Though long before thy hand they touch
I know that they must withered be
But yet reject them not as such[4]

1    This letter was in the same envelope as that of the previous letter, also apparently written on 28 February 1904.

2    There are signs of pressed roses in the letter.

3    The Reeses probably ran a boarding house. George Reese is listed in the 1910 census as living in Pittsburgh's eleventh ward with his wife Cathryne, two granddaughters, a grandson and five non-relatives.

4    Annie sent some pressed roses with her letter. The lines are imperfectly recalled from
the second stanza of Ben Jonson's 'To Celia'.

———————

6 MARCH 1904
[Hotel Royal Palm stationery
Biscayne Bay, Miami, Florida]
Sunday night

My dear Jim,

Your last letter reached me on Wednesday last and I am glad to see you are doing nicely and that you are not lonely. I had letter from Pollie, and I think there are a few that would like *James* a little nearer to them than Pittsburgh, but it appears the family will soon be united again as Pollie says we will soon see each other.

There is not a thing new here, beautiful, bright sunny days and lots of pleasure for those who can take it all in, but we are perfectly happy in our own way. We have the children and our work to do, and it seems to me we enjoy it as much as the wealthiest of them sitting around.

These last few days were very nice not too hot and yesterday morning as I was sitting in the shade of a tall coconut tree, a large coconut fell within a yard of me. It was Providence saved me, for if it had struck me, I would have been killed. As soon as those large nuts ripen, they drop and woe be to the one they fall on.

Well, Mr. Mellon is not yet with us and may not be for a long time, so our folks are going out on the boat for ten days and leave us here. They have quite a party of Pittsburghers here and will have them as guests of the *Vagabondia*, so maybe after all when Mr. M. comes, we may not stay so long at this hotel.

I sincerely hope we will get home soon after Easter Sunday. Won't that be nice just to have you there. I will not be looking for a letter this time on my arrival but for you yourself. How often do I think when I am alone of where we shall meet. I know you will soon be quite familiar with the different streets.

I had a dream where you met me and gave me a small parcel; yet, it seemed as though I couldn't talk to you, so Rose handed me the parcel. I untied it and found it to contain a few leaden things like a saucer with Indianapolis marked in large letters on each one. Then I showed them to Ellen, and while so doing, I heard the boat coming in and woke up only to find I was still in Miami.

I wonder if you have seen Rose. At least I hope so. She would be likely to call at the hotel, but you know Mary is not at all what she appeared to you. One Sunday evening when Mr. and Mrs. Connor and your uncle were out at the Mellon house, she was anything but nice. I am afraid if you should go there, she wouldn't be very nice to you, but then if Mrs. Walters and Rose were there, I do know you would certainly be welcome if you feel like going out there before we get back. First telephone them. I don't know why they don't write to us as I wrote to Mrs. W. and Ellen to Rose, but as yet have not heard a word from them.

I wonder, Jim, if you brought all my letters with you. At least I hope not. If you did, I want you to promise you won't tease me about them. My little girl was writing something today. She told me to get a pencil and write to Jim. That I didn't write to him for so long, so you see if I should happen to forget you, some one is sure to mention your name.

Well, dear Jim, I wish I were with you tonight and when such cannot be, you have my thoughts and best love always and don't get too busy to remember me sometimes. Write long letters and give my kindest regards to your uncle and remember me to all, so now must finish.

Good night, and I remain
fondly Annie xxxxxx

16 MARCH 1904
[Hotel Royal Palm stationery
Biscayne Bay, Miami, Florida[1]]
March 16, 1904

My dear Jim,

Your letter reached me this morning and how glad I was to see the postmark that you were still in Pittsburgh, not that I don't wish you to go to Philadelphia, but it seems you would be nearer where you now are. The one thing is I hope you will be right in Pittsburgh when I get home. It would be so nice to see the Quarries and Miss Hearty, and I do wonder what they will say to you, and if you will tell them about me.[2] You know I would like so much to be remembered to them all.

I am glad you called on Mary, but I think it strange they didn't know you were in town as I am positive I wrote them you were coming, and they answered they were glad. It would be so much nicer for us, but I am not sure that I told them any more after that.

Well, Jim, I was never so surprised as when I read about the Jap. I think he is too forward going to Mrs. C[onnor?] so often and Mrs. C never said anything about him in her letters, but I think she should know Ellen by this to have any doubt about her, and whilst poor Ellen did everything as she thought for the best. Still, you see she is the one to suffer, but long before this, I talked it over with Ellen. I know she never would think of going out with him if it hadn't been that he asked her to take him to our Church, and she couldn't refuse. Beyond that there was nothing more, for Rose and Mrs. Walters went out with him as often as Ellen. Rose and Ellen and I were the only ones to help him out when he first came, but it seems as if he imposed more on Ellen's good nature than on ours. Mary was so awful mean to him that he needed some one to have a kind word sometime for him. I have told Ellen over and over not to be so foolish just to let people do something for themselves, but she didn't see it that way till it was too late. She is too good-hearted, but I think she will not be so much so for the future. It doesn't do. I think it was very nice of you, Jim, to let me know as we don't ever need to mention it, but yet know what is going on.

Well, I am sorry to hear Pollie is not well, but I hope it is not serious. I knew your uncle would be kept pretty busy, yet, I thought it would be nice to write him as I said I would. He will write soon I hope.

Mr. Mellon is not coming till 19th or 20th, so we are still in the dark about leaving here. Yet, I do believe we will be in Pittsburgh about the 15th April.

I believe, Jim, that Reese's is about the most expensive place you could find as you see they have high rent to pay and must charge accordingly. There is nobody makes more money in Pittsburgh than those keeping roomers or boarders and the Brennans will find it costly to live here. Of course, it was very home-like at Reese's, but your bill runs high. It would be better for you to get some place that would room and board you. Where you stayed when you came before was, of course, an expensive place too, but they give two meals. The trouble is you have to go away out to the East End away from the city before you can get any kind of a place to stay. For your sake, I wish the Brennans would come. It would be so much better.

I see you too like pretty picture frames. That's one of my fancies. I love nice pictures and frames.

Well, I wonder what you will do on the 17th tomorrow. I know you will miss Indianapolis then. We are going to have all the Irish airs played and 'St. Patrick's dance' in the evening whilst for dessert we will have 'St. Patrick's Punch', so you see we have no room for complaining.

I wonder if this will reach you in Philadelphia. Won't you have a good time talking of our old trip, and I wonder if they will know you. Perhaps a good many of them are married. Even so, try and find them. If there is anything you would want me to know, don't wait till Sunday to write. Just write when you can, and rest assured that I trust you to the end and always will. I can not think of you as anything else but good. Your nice letters are always bright and comforting, but it seems as if I can't do anything for you in return. You have always my first and last thought after my prayers and the best love I can give, I am your fondest,

    A xxxxx

1   Letter was sent to Mr James P. Phelan, General Delivery, Philadelphia, Pa.

2   The Quarries and Miss Hearty may have been friends of the Brennans or residents in the house where Jim stayed.

---

## 21 MARCH 1904

[Envelope contains one rose pressed in the paper of the Hotel Royal Palm. There is no message.][1]

1   Envelope postmarked Pittsburgh, March 21, 1904. Florida postmark torn. Letter sent c/o Joseph Brennan, Colonial Hotel, was forwarded to Jim c/o General Delivery, Philadelphia, Pa.

---

## 24 MARCH 1904

                   [*Vagabondia* stationery[1]]

                   March 24th, 1904

My dear Jim,

Mr. Mellon came here on Sunday last and took us all on the boat early on Monday, but we are now going right back again to the hotel, and Mr. Mellon is going to Texas again.[2] We will leave the Royal Palm on Sunday 27th and go as far north as St. Augustine where we will stay till Mr. M. comes. Then we will go on board the boat for a short trip before going home.

Now, doesn't that sound good? Just think of moving north even if it takes a few weeks more to get home. Still, it is a consolation to know that we are getting nearer home at last. The weather is fearful hot here now, and I am so glad to know we are going to where we will have a chance of being at least a little cooler as St. Augustine is more than a night's ride by rail north of Miami. The boat goes north by ocean. We expect Mr. M. back from Texas again by the first of April. It all depends on him how soon we may be able to get home.

I know your last Sunday's letter will be waiting for me at the hotel, and I am so anxious to know where you are now and if you are doing well. I have the meanest pen but will only write a few lines just to let you know our whereabouts.

Since Monday last we have visited some of the best fishing places in the country, and it is beautiful on the water these moonlight lights. We are doing nicely and would feel ever so much better if we were going home. St. Augustine is a beautiful city just full of interest, and I am glad we are going there.

So now, dear Jim, hoping you and the friends are well, I will finish for this time. Remember me to your uncle. I haven't heard from him. Will write you again as soon as we get to St. Augustine.

With love as ever Anniexxxx

1 Letter forwarded to No.2 Mint Area[?], Philadelphia
2 W. L. Mellon became Executive Vice-President of Guffey Petroleum in 1902. The oil business took W. L. to Texas frequently as the Mellons took over controlling interest. The corporation was reorganised in 1907 as the Gulf Oil Corporation. W. L. resigned as Chairman of the Board of Gulf in 1948. Hersh, *Mellon Family*, pp. 121–2, 449.

28 MARCH 1904

[*Vagabondia* stationery[1]]
We will have the same address.
Hotel Royal P.
Miami, Fla.
March 28th, 1904

My dear Jim,

Your letter reached me yesterday just as I had come home from Church. In my last letter I told you we were going to St. Augustine, but we are not. There is an entirely new plan now. The trouble is these people don't know their own minds for one day, so instead we are going to Cuba and Key West and *must* leave here for Pittsburgh on the 14th April as Mr. Mellon has to be in Pittsburgh before the 18th.

You can write till about the 11th but not any later, and do please, Jim, let me have a few letters when we come back here again. As you see, we will leave Miami today and come back about the 14th and start north right away.

I knew the Walton paper at once as we stayed there a few times.[1] Don't you think it is a nice hotel? My! but your letter was looked for. I didn't know what had happened and was afraid I should leave here ere I got it. Just think, next Sunday is Easter and goodness knows we might be miles away from any church, so I want you to say a few prayers for me.

Perhaps this will be the last letter I may have a chance of writing you, but if I can, I will write even a few lines. Isn't it grand to think we are so soon to see each other? The time will not be long in passing, and I know I'll be glad. I wonder when will you get back to Pittsburgh again. I will lose no time in going down to see you when I get home. Of course I must wait till evening, but you telephone on the 18th and Mrs. Walters will be sure to know when we will arrive. We always send a telegram. Then I can call you up or you me some time during the way.

We had a letter from Rose yesterday. *She* will be so glad to have us home. She was telling me of a fine Japanese sale they were having in Wood St. and I wished I were there as she got some nice things herself and so did the other girls.[2]

Well now, Jim, as I have told you nearly everything, I will finish and will ask you as a special favour to write as soon as you get this and another one before the 11th which will be the last for this time. I hope you will succeed in finding our friends. I will be very anxious to hear of them. I wonder if your uncle is back yet and how Pollie is. If I have a chance I will write to him ere we go home. Now, Jim, with best love to you and hoping all will be well and see you soon.

I remain as ever fondly Annie xxxxx

1   Letter sent c/o Mr McLaughlin, 1228 Summer Street, Philadelphia, Pa.
2   Annie may have stayed at the Walton Hotel on her way to or from Spring Lake.
3   Like many Irish domestic servants, Annie's experience in the Mellon's household developed her appreciation for the decorative arts.

———————

1 APRIL 1904
[Hotel Royal Palm stationery[1]
Biscayne Bay, Florida]
April 1, 1904[2]

My dear Jim,
We are going back to Miami today which will be the last time till we go there two weeks from today to go home, so this will really be my last letter *unless* any other plan turns up when Mr. Mellon comes tomorrow.

We called at Miami on Wednesday last and wasn't I glad to get your nice letter. Maybe I didn't think you were nice not to disappoint me. I mailed you a letter on Monday and hope you got it all right. I suppose you are still at the *Walton* and wonder if you will be there long now. You see we will soon be home, and isn't that fine. I had a nice letter from the old man [Jim's uncle Joseph Brennan], and I am sorry to see that Pollie has been real sick. He is in Pittsburgh again and the family will be there soon. I wonder where they will locate. I hope it will be somewhere in the East End as I am sure you will stay with them.

I had a letter from Mrs. Walters some time ago and she said John Brennan was married. I thought probably she was joking me so I never wrote you anything about it as she writes the jolliest letters. You tell me if it is so.

I want you to go out and see the girls as soon as you have an opportunity after you come back and call at my sisters too. Drop them a line just a day or so before going in as they retire too early, and I would like you to see the Lydon children. If you write to them just two days ahead, as I do, they will make you some nice raisin bread that I love, and think of me when you are having a cup of tea with them. You will find them real hard to make friends with but wait till I come home. You will not have so hard a time.

Well, we are having a nice time here just out on the beach and fishing, but we are fearfully sunburned. My face today is so very red and sore. We go to bed early at night but are up just at day break in the morning. It is nice for us. We are having a good rest anyhow.

I don't wonder you are not in love with Philadephia, for I never was. I am glad you like Pittsburgh better. I believe you will make that your home yet. Don't forget to call on Mrs. Connor. She will be glad to see you. I am sorry she has not been well either. It has been a cold winter and the poor have suffered much. It is well we escaped it, but you know I don't mind the cold at all.

Well now, dear Jim, I must finish and don't forget to write on the days I said in my last letter, and be sure to telephone Mrs. Walters about our coming. I wonder where we will meet. It will be just where *you* say. Now I will give you my sister's address:

Mrs. P. Lyons
Rear of 1225 Liberty Street
Pittsburgh, Pa

You write to her, and if you would like to see them before I go home, it would be real nice as they would like to know you a little more so as to tease me some. As yet, they don't know what to do. Now, good-bye, Jim, and won't I be the happiest thing to leave here for home, dear house with you to see me.

I am as ever
Your fondest Annie xxxx

1   Letter sent care of Mr. McLaughlin, 1228 Summer St., Philadelphia, Pa.
2   There is a break between Annie's letter from Miami on 1 April 1904 and 7 June 1904.

---

7 JUNE 1904

Tuesday morning
[No return address. Postmarked June 7, 1904[1]]

My dear Jim,

I got your letter a few minutes ago and what a relief it was to know you are still living. You will never know the agony I suffered since last Saturday evening when your uncle called me up and asked where Jim was. I thought he was joking and passed it off, but when you didn't meet me on Saturday night at church I became anxious and went to see your aunt on Sunday evening. She was sure you met with an accident and oh! how I dreaded the thoughts of of it.

We talked of you all the time, and I am afraid you will get a scolding when you come back, but don't you get angry as you know it was a wrong thing for you to go away and not let anyone know where you were going. I am not mad with you, Jim. I am too glad to hear from you and forgive easily and will be more anxious than ever to see you. Well might you picture me with a wet handkerchief, yes, and more than one, but I will tell you all when I see you, and Jim, do hurry up and come as soon as you can. Don't ever run away with the idea that I like you better far away. You know that is *not* so.

Well now that's about all I will say. You will get no more scolding from me, for I will be too glad to see you. Do hurry up and come. I will stay in every night this week so you can come right out here and I will not take as long to come down stairs as the night I was washing my hair. Telephone me as soon as you come here. Give my love to Pollie and all and lots of it for yourself. I am

As ever,
Your old Annie xxxx

1   Letter sent to 702 South West Street, Indianapolis, Ind.

---

20 JUNE 1904

[No return address.
Postmarked E. Liberty Station
Pittsburgh, Pa.]
June 20, 1904[1]

My dear Jim,

What on earth is the matter that you don't write and tell me something? It is now two weeks since I got your letter saying you would be back at the end of the week. From that time have I been patiently waiting for your return. Not even a few lines just to break this cruel suspense. Well might you know at this one time in our lives that I would worry about your absence, but if things have not gone for you as you wished, why not let me know? Did you not know a long time ago that I would try to make it easier for you if possible?

Now the time for my leaving these people is very near and I must know something from you before I will make any further plans. so answer this at once and say when you expect to be here.[2]

Mrs. B has been real sick, saw her last night and she looked badly.

Do wire or write soon as you can and tell me what the trouble is as I am and will be just as faithful to you in your troubles as I would be in prosperity only don't keep me any longer waiting to know just what is wrong. I am worried half to death since you left, so don't know what is coming next

Now I am

as ever your faithful

Annie xx.

1   Letter sent Special Delivery to 702 South West St. Indianapolis, Indiana. Envelope stamped 'Addressee not at . . .'. In pencil on the back of the envelope: Moved to about 412 New Jersey, 6/20/04.

2   It is not clear when Annie left the Mellon household and whether she worked or only stayed with Mrs. Malzell who has not been identified.

---

25 JUNE 1904

Wednesday

[No return address.

Postmarked TR3 Pittsburgh,

June 25, 1904[1]]

My dear Jim,

I have often thought of you all day and hoped each hour would bring me some news from you. I am sure you must have my telegram and [know] how anxious I am to know if you are soon coming but would be very pleased indeed if you could get along there as I know it would be as good if not better than Pittsburgh but then you know best and I do hope you will succeed in getting something suitable. You like Indianapolis better I am sure than any other city, and therefore, you would feel better contented than here with twice as much and you know my liking for it, so that will not put you back as I can make myself at home anywhere *you* are.

If you make up your mind to stay, I see no reason why you would have to come for me as I could go whenever you got ready for me. Mrs. Malzell has asked me to stay till Tuesday next and I don't know where I may go then, but I will surely hear from you before then. You didn't say if you got any of my letters and am now wondering if they ever reached you.

Well, Jim, I am glad you got out of the saloon, for I know it caused you more worry than enough, so now you can settle to something else. I was glad to get your letter as I could not imagine what had become of you nor why you did not write. Well, I am still looking for you, and everytime the phone rings I imagine it is for me. By this time the mailman has his own ideas but is very consoling always saying, 'Well, the next mail will surely bring you one'.

Mrs. B. certainly had a mean spell but is feeling all right now and Earl is anxious to know if I have given up the trip to Ireland. He is a great boy.[2]

I am glad you are having a nice time there and 'are you sure it was your brother's wife you had with you?' Many times have I passed by the old stopping place, near our street, and wondered if we will ever say 'good night' there again. I felt lonely coming home alone each time I have gone out but hope to soon hear from you and then I can do a good deal more. So, Jim, do write me very soon and tell me what you want me to do.

I saw Rose a few nights ago and what a nice chat we had principally about Jim. Several others have inquired about him but must hunt up some other source for minute details as I will not give them. So now Jim, won't you write just as soon as you get this and let me know all and I am and ever will be

with love your fondest Annie xxxxxxx

1    Letter sent to 315 South New Jersey Street, Indianapolis, Indiana
2    While it sounds as though Earl was Annie's nephew, neither Bridget nor Mary had a son called Earl. He may have been one of the Brennans.

---

27 JUNE 1904

Monday
[No return address.
Postmarked East Liberty Station
June 27, 1904[1]]

My dear Jim,

Another Sunday has come and gone and you don't seem a bit nearer. Now I am at a loss to know just what I will do as tomorrow will be my last day here, but the lady has asked me to stay as long as I could with her but she will leave here on Thursday. When I got your last letter I surely thought you would be here on Friday night, and how I did wait for you, but goodness knows how many more nights I must wait. If I only knew just what to do I wouldn't mind, but as I am, it is just hard to say anything now. I don't know if you will settle down here when you come or if you will want to wait a while longer. Of course, Jim, it is just as you wish it. Only if I knew, I wouldn't worry, as you see after this week I will not be working and that means a good deal of expense.

Mrs. B. wants me to spend a few days with her, so when you come back you will find me either here or with the Brennans. Mrs. B. has been my only friend since you left, and I certainly will not forget her.

I want you to *wire* me just as soon as you get this if only a few words to say what you are doing. If you do it right away, it will reach me here.

Wednesday will be the 29th June. What does that remind you of?[2] If you had stayed here, I'm sure we would both be more interested in looking for it, but perhaps it was all for the best as there is another 29th.

I am writing this under difficulties so excuse the mistakes. Now, Jim, I will ask you please wire me as soon as you get this. Tell me what to do and when you are coming. I wish you were going to settle down there and send for me. Then I would be happy as that was always the height of my ambition.

Well, I must hurry as the postman is coming and don't worry about the pin. If everything was as easily remedied, it would be easy. I will replace it. Now let me know as soon as you can. I am waiting. The same address will find me. So now, dear Jim, must finish with ever fondest love to you, am your old Annie

1    Letter sent Special Delivery to 315 South New Jersey St. Indianapolis, Ind. Address crossed out on front. Written in purple pencil on the verso of the envelope is Mr. James Phelan, 5th House from Perryville Avenue on Charles St., Allegheny, Pa. The Phelans eventually settled on Dunlap Street off Perrysville Avenue.
2    Jim wrote to Annie first on 29 June 1901

✦

## EPILOGUE

Postcard of the S.S. *Celtic* posted from Spiddal, County Galway, 23 June 1911 to James Phelan, Dunlap Av., N.S., Pittsburgh, Pa. Address crossed out 88 Charles.

Dear Dada:
This is the boat we came to Ireland on. Keep all these postals for an album when we get back. We are in Lippa now and John is writing this.

Son & Mother